THE SOUTH ASIA STORY

THE SOUTH ASIA STORY

THE FIRST SIXTY YEARS
OF US RELATIONS WITH INDIA
AND PAKISTAN

HAROLD A. GOULD

Los Angeles | London | New Delhi
Singapore | Washington DC | Melbourne

First published in 2010 by

 SAGE Publications India Pvt Ltd
B1/I-1, Mohan Cooperative Industrial Area
Mathura Road, New Delhi 110 044, India
www.sagepub.in

SAGE Publications Inc
2455 Teller Road
Thousand Oaks, California 91320, USA

SAGE Publications Ltd
1 Oliver's Yard, 55 City Road
London EC1Y 1SP, United Kingdom

SAGE Publications Asia-Pacific Pte Ltd
3 Church Street
#10-04 Samsung Hub
Singapore 049483

Published by Vivek Mehra for SAGE Publications India Pvt Ltd, typeset in 12/17pt Garamond Premier Pro by Star Compugraphics Private Limited, Delhi.

Library of Congress Cataloging-in-Publication Data Available

ISBN: 978-81-321-0121-5 (PB)

The SAGE Team: Rekha Natarajan, Nawazish Azim,
Meena Chakravorty, Sanjeev Kumar Sharma,
and Trinankur Banerjee
Photo Credit: Public Affairs Section, U.S. Embassy, New Delhi, India

Contents

List of Photographs

PRELUDE

THE SOUTH ASIAN POLICIES OF AMERICAN PRESIDENTS

T his series of articles was written at the behest of the late Mr Gopal Raju, editor-in-chief of *News India-Times*. They appeared in this magazine in twelve installments from February 16 to May 11, 2007. In a slightly revised form, they now have been assembled in this small volume. As with the original pieces, the purpose was and is to provide brief sketches of how each U.S. president since Franklin Roosevelt perceived and dealt with South Asia—most particularly, of course, India and Pakistan. The essays are deliberately succinct and assiduously avoid ponderous and technical phraseology while nevertheless striving to present an authoritative yet readable account of the course that

U.S. South Asian policy has followed over the past sixty years. In fact, clarity and readability, combined with an abundance of archival photographs to enliven the text and stimulate visual awareness of the historical events adumbrated, have been the prime motivation; the hope is that this format will arouse the interest of informed citizens and induce them to acquire greater understanding of this crucially important but frequently misunderstood region.

The rise of politicized Islam and terrorism has raised the strategic ante in South Asia to an unprecedented level. Prior to the Soviet invasion of Afghanistan and the Muslim ultra-radicalism which this has in turn spawned, South Asia did not occupy a high priority status either in the eyes of the American public or the country's foreign policy establishment. Very little effort was made to develop scholarly expertise and linguistic competence on South and Southeast Asia. Only a few American universities maintained any semblance of so-called area studies programs focused on these regions; even today there are no more than a dozen of such programs, of mixed quality, in the entire country.

Now, however, there is at last a realization that South Asia matters in the larger scheme of things. It can be said that Pakistan is the original home base of contemporary terrorism and jihadism. Driven by conflict over Kashmir and communal antipathy that has dogged Hindu–Muslim relationships for more than a century, India and Pakistan have lived perennially on the threshold of ethno-religious war. Due to its proximity to Afghanistan, Pakistan has become an involuntary host of both Al Qaeda and the Taliban; Mullah Umar and Osama bin Laden have been asylumed for years somewhere along the Afghan–Pakistan border. Terrorist attacks emanating from Pakistan have targeted Kashmir, as well as major Indian urban centers like Mumbai, Hyderabad, and Delhi, for over twenty years. The horrific "26–11" attack on Mumbai by Lashkar-i-Tayiba is merely the latest manifestation of Pakistan's obsessive aversion to India.

Nuclear proliferation and the threat of nuclear war has also become a fact of life in South Asia. Ironically, so has the global economy. The power to destroy and the power to prosper walk hand in hand in the region.

It all comes down to the fact that America, and indeed the world, cannot any longer take South Asia lightly. For this reason, it is important to understand the region's historical roots, the crises and challenges its people and governments have faced, and the region's triumphs and tragedies. Hopefully this small volume will help to achieve a measure of this needed understanding.

There have been twelve American presidents, from World War II until the present, who have left their imprint on the region. Each will be considered chronologically: 1. Franklin D. Roosevelt (1941–1945); 2. Harry S. Truman (1945–1953); 3. Dwight D. Eisenhower (1953–1961); 4. John F. Kennedy (1961–1963); 5. Lyndon

Baines Johnson (1963–1969); 6. Richard M. Nixon (1969–1974); 7. Gerald Ford (1974–1977); 8. Jimmy Carter (1977–1981); 9. Ronald Reagan (1981–1989); 10. George H.W. Bush (1989–1993); 11. Bill Clinton (1993–2001); 12. George W. Bush (2001–2009). In point of fact, as of November 4, 2008, we must now add a thirteenth American president, Barack Hussein Obama, to our list of American presidents, whose mandate has just commenced and whose impact now awaits the judgment of history.

During this same period there have been fourteen Indian prime ministers: 1. Jawaharlal Nehru (1947–1964); 2. Gulzari Lal Nanda (1964); 3. Lal Bahadur Shastri (1964–1966); 4.&6. Indira Gandhi (1966–1977/1980–1984); 5. Morarji Desai (1977–1979); 7. Charan Singh (1979–1980); 8. Rajiv Gandhi (1984–1989); 9. V.P. Singh (1989–1990); 10. Chandra Shekhar (1990–1991); 11. P.V. Narasimha Rao (1991–1996); 12.&15. Atal Behari Vajpayee (1996/1998–2004); 13. H.D. Deve Gowda (1996–1997); 14. I.K. Gujral (1997); 16. Manmohan Singh (2004–present).

There are, of course, broad historical patterns, which underlie the individual actions and define the context of these presidents; but their unique personalities, levels of awareness, and intellectual gifts (or lack of them!) inevitably played an important role in what use they made of the options that history and immediate circumstances conferred on them. World War II and its immediate aftermath presented unique challenges. The permutations and ramifications of the Cold War posed the most sustained challenges to the first nine presidents—that is, Roosevelt through Reagan. Following the end of the Cold War, the rise of Islamic radicalism and terrorism has occupied center stage. However, Kashmir and Indo-Pakistani enmity has been a common thread running through all eras and presidencies, including even the most recent turn in U.S.–Indian relations toward greater political amity and formal strategic collaboration.

It needs to be pointed out that none of these American presidents ever had any meaningful experience with South Asia prior to entering office. For all of them it was a matter of "on-the-job training." How they coped with this obviously varied in accordance with their individual political gifts and their ideological predisposition. Richard Nixon, for example, was ill-disposed toward India from the outset of his administration for reasons that are given in Chapter 6. Dwight D. Eisenhower (Chapter 3), Nixon's original "boss," was increasingly drawn toward friendlier feelings toward India after having developed warm personal feelings for Jawaharlal Nehru. John F. Kennedy (Chapter 4), on the other hand, gravitated from idealism toward a measure of skepticism and disenchantment after he personally encountered Nehru during the prime minister's declining years. Lyndon Johnson (Chapter 5) developed an ambivalent attitude toward Indira Gandhi after she criticized his

Vietnam policy. Bill Clinton's (Chapter 11) remarkable political instincts and sharp intellect, abetted by a boost from Pakistani political psychopathology, transformed him into a "convert" to the idea of comprehensive U.S.–Indian rapprochement. George Bush-2 (Chapter 12) became the unlikely architect of the final achievement of that rapprochement. It has now become President Barack Obama's challenge to synthesize and refine the positive achievements of his twelve predecessors and complete the process of fulfilling the quest for amity and mutual respect that began over sixty years ago.

We now must wait and see what the future holds for U.S.–Indian relations as the next regime change in U.S. politics commences.

Acknowledgements

I wish to thank the late Mr Gopal Raju, Editor & Publisher of *News India-Times* for inviting me to publish the series of twelve articles on how U.S. presidents dealt with South Asia from World War II to the present upon which this book is based. Also I wish to express my gratitude to Senior Editor Ms Ela Dutt, of *News India-Times*, who so expertly guided me through the manifold editorial and other tasks connected with getting these articles into print. I want to express my gratitude to the SAGE Team (Rekha Natarajan, Nawazish Azim, and Meena Chakravorty) who helped and guided me through the permutations of this enterprise, along with Aarti David (Senior Assistant Manager, PR) and Subir Lahiri (Production Manager), and many others.

Finally I want to offer a special thanks to my dear friend and colleague, Dr T.N. Madan, of the Institute for Economic Growth, for his help and support in guiding this book through to publication. Also, special thanks to Ambassador Harry K. Thomas, Jr., Executive Secretary, U.S. Department of State, for encouraging me to publish these articles in book form.

1

WORLD WAR II AND THE ROOSEVELT ADMINISTRATION

Consciousness of South Asia actually originated during World War II, considerably prior to the dawning of the postwar era. In the end, of course, the basis for everything became the Cold War. The latter occurred only after important "regime changes" had taken place both in the United States and South Asia. In the United States the change can be said to have been "intramural": from the New Deal liberals who had been politically dominant throughout the Great Depression and most of World War II to a

Trumanesque breed of conventional, balance-of-power hard-liners who rose to prominence after the death of Franklin D. Roosevelt in 1945. In South Asia, the change was both "extramural" and "intramural": from the British *Raj* to political independence, and from an unitary subcontinental geopolitical entity to a politically subdivided Subcontinent consisting of the two separate states of India and Pakistan.

Out of these transformations emerged new political realities, which profoundly shaped relations between America and the Indic world for the ensuing six decades, affecting in turn every subsequent U.S. administration.

India, under the Congress Party, led by Jawaharlal Nehru and the spirit of Mahatma Gandhi, would adopt liberal democracy, secularism, a Socialist idiom for economic development, and a so-called non-aligned approach to international relations. Pakistan, led by the Muslim League and Muhammad Ali Jinnah, would establish itself as an "Islamic state" governed by a "viceregal" political system,[1] with a quasi-capitalist economy, a polity controlled by traditional landlords, a colonial-era bureaucratic elite, and a Punjabi-dominated military establishment. Both countries were born in an atmosphere of ethno-religious conflict and a perpetual state of mutual hostility over entitlement to the former princely state of Jammu and Kashmir.

At the core of the doctrinal synthesis that evolved in the United States at this time was an obsessive preoccupation with the spread of world communism, first in its Soviet incarnation and subsequently in its Chinese incarnation as well. As the 1940s drew to a close, this threat structure had become the *raison d'être* of U.S. foreign policy. America's strategic response was the doctrine of "containment," or the establishment of a *cordon sanitaire* around the entire perimeter of the communist world, from East and Inner Asia to Central and Eastern Europe, through a complex of military alliances. It was the rationale behind the *Marshall Plan*[2] and the creation of *NATO*[3] in Europe. It impelled the so-called *Truman Doctrine* that opposed communist-led insurgency in Greece.[4] It was the reason why America went to war on the Korean peninsula.[5] It subsequently led to the Bay of Pigs,[6] to Vietnam, to Iran-Contra,[7] and many other interventions around the world. It was, of course, the reason why American policy-makers cast their postwar strategic gaze toward South Asia in the first place and eventually led them to the conclusion that the militarized grand strategy they had crafted for other parts of the world was appropriate here as well. Eventually this led to the establishment of *CENTO* and *SEATO*, the two treaty systems that ineluctably drew the region into the mainstream of the Cold War,[8] and in the process, I contend, doomed America's South Asia policy to eventual failure.

Out of the public debate that determined America's approach to South Asia, came a regional strategy with five explicit aims: (*i*) to prevent communist bloc penetration from outside the region, (*ii*) to deter the rise of domestic communism within the region, (*iii*) to prevent intraregional war between India and Pakistan over Kashmir or indeed any other precipitant, (*iv*) to promote economic development throughout the Subcontinent based upon free-market economics, and (*v*) to encourage the evolution and preservation of democratic political institutions.

At the earliest point of significant contact between India and the United States, and even for a brief time following World War II, however, the martial scenario for controlling events in South Asia had not achieved the dominant standing in the policy-making domain that subsequently proved to be the case. The point when it became the dominant motif goes back to the already alluded to factional cleavage between the New Deal liberals and the more conservative wing of the Democratic party that occurred around the time of President Franklin D. Roosevelt's nomination for a fourth term.

This conflict was inherent in the struggle over who should be selected as Roosevelt's running mate for vice-president. The liberals' choice was the incumbent vice-president, Henry Agard Wallace, who advocated radical social and economic change both at home and abroad, versus the conservatives' choice, Senator Harry S. Truman, who represented a more conventional approach to both domestic and foreign policy. When the latter faction won out, and when after Roosevelt's death in 1945, followed by the accession of Harry S. Truman to the presidency, the stage was set for a showdown over postwar foreign policy. The Yalta summit meeting in February 1945 had churned up great controversy among the American political establishment over whether too much had been conceded to Stalin in the run-up to the impending postwar political process. The advisors upon whom Truman increasingly relied were primarily foreign policy hawks emanating from the conservative wing of the party, who viewed the impending postwar world order with alarm. They believed that the victorious Soviet Union and the powerful Red Army were poised to pursue a relentless course of world conquest, employing Marxist–Leninist doctrines as their ideological shibboleth.

With respect to South Asia, however, importantly because of Roosevelt's and other New Dealers' anti-colonialist predilections, the United States was favor-ably disposed toward the emergence of nationalism in the Indian Subcontinent and indeed other parts of the globe as well (for example, Southeast Asia, especially Vietnam and Indonesia). It was seen as a promising trend toward some form of political autonomy coupled with democracy for India and other former colonial states once the war ended, which might be a model for postcolonial nations everywhere. Had postwar American foreign policy continued in this spirit after the war ended and shown deeper understanding and appreciation of Nehru's determination to create a bulwark against political extremism and totalitarianism by making India a viable, peaceful democracy, while maintaining neutrality between the two emergent global power blocs, the Cold War might well have been kept out of the region.

But this was not to be once the policy hawks won the day in the United States.

2

THE TRUMAN ADMINISTRATION (1945–1953)

While the Truman administration represented, as mentioned in Chapter 1, a transition from the more idealistic, "one-world," anticolonialist orientation of the Roosevelt administration to a more conventional balance-of-power-style global politics, the period from 1945 to 1952, like any genuinely transitional phase, was not a monolith; it revealed an admixture of seemingly contradictory trends.

There was the convening of the San Francisco Conference in March–April of 1945, which created the United Nations, in principle certainly one of the most idealistic political endeavors in human history. Yet, its charter and composition went only part way toward providing a forum where social injustices like colonialism and racism could be fully eradicated from the world. Attesting to this was the refusal of the conference's organizers to replace Great Britain's hand-picked mouthpieces for the traditional *Raj* (Sir Feroze Shah Noon, Sir Ramaswamy Mudaliar, V.L. Krishnamachari) with Jawaharlal Nehru's sister, Madame Vijayalakshmi Pandit, as demanded by the *Indian National Congress* and the *"India Lobby"* in the United States, to be the *bona fide* representative of soon-to-be-independent India.[1] By 1950, the United States was at war in Korea, attempting ostensibly in the name of the United Nations to prevent North Korea from communizing the entire Korean peninsula.[2] This was an aspect of a now well established global grand strategy, stretching from Western Europe to Mainland China, whose declared purpose was "containing Communism."

South Asia was gradually being drawn into this grand strategy by virtue of three factors: (*i*) Nehru's unwillingness to join the Western Alliance, despite his predilection for Westminster democracy; (*ii*) Pakistan's corresponding willingness to join the Grand Alliance by feigning anticommunism as a means of acquiring enough military power and diplomatic support to wrest control of Kashmir; and (*iii*) the success, which Sir Olaf Caroe (Foreign Secretary for the pre-Independence Government of India) and other traditional British Great Game imperialists achieved in persuading a largely historically naive body of nascent postwar American policy-makers to incorporate newly created Pakistan into a contemplated *cordon sanitaire* around an expansive Soviet Union (see Caroe 1958).[3] Taken together, these factors inclined the Truman Administration toward viewing South Asia in conventional power-politics terms.

Caroe was the leader of the "Great Game faction" of British officials, who wanted Partition to achieve a "Greater Pakistan" that maximally encompassed all of the frontier provinces—as well as much of the Punjab as could be obtained, plus Baluchistan, up to the Durand Line facing Afghanistan, the North Western Frontier Province (NWFP) and Kashmir. They envisioned a strategic structure that would preserve as much as possible the "Great Game model," which had been the basis for British imperial policy for more than a century prior to Partition and Independence.

Caroe was instinctively oriented toward what would become the Cold War grand strategy promulgated by the United States, its British ally, and other Western states as they were primed for inclusion in the anti-Soviet crusade under the rubric of *NATO*. He had numerous contacts with the emerging circle of American Cold Warriors who were moving into key policy-making positions in the Truman administration by 1948. They were searching for insight into regions like South and Southwest Asia, which had perennially lain outside the historical purview of the

United States. This was especially the case with South Asia about which Americans knew virtually nothing. It was natural for them to look to British officials, especially those with both civilian and military backgrounds in the colonial administration, who purportedly were knowledgeable about the strategic vicissitudes of the South Asian region.

The Americans were enticed to favor a "greater Pakistan" that included Kashmir because their Brit imperial mentors dangled before them the prospects of establishing an American airbase in the Kashmir Valley if the province were incorporated in Pakistan. In the end, of course, the Americans were able to establish a spy-plane and listening post base in Peshawar.

Men like Caroe told them what their own backgrounds had preconditioned them to resonate with. They were driven by conventional power-politics of the old school, as were their British mentors, and had no feel whatsoever for the rising tide of alternative non-aligned perspectives on the international environment, which emergent nationalist movements were generating.

Yet, even as this trend was establishing itself, the Truman administration made another decision that pointed, in its potential implications, at least, in quite the opposite direction. This was the appointment of Chester Bowles, one of the last of the prominent New Dealers, as Ambassador to India in 1951. Essentially, Bowles opposed the militarization of America's South

Asia policy, especially the incorporation of Pakistan into the West's alliance system against the Soviet Union, because he believed this would make her a destabilizing force in the region. He got on famously with Jawaharlal Nehru, who he believed was an authentic democrat in the liberal tradition who with sensible American diplomatic support and economic assistance would prevent India from going communist (allegedly the principal goal of U.S. policy), and make her a bulwark against the rising tide of totalitarianism that was threatening the newly free nations of the world. This could be accomplished, Bowles believed, by simply assuring Nehru's political survival, and what he stood for, despite his determination to keep India "non-aligned" and available as a mediatory Third Force between the two rival power blocs.

Bowles stated the case extremely well. "How silly we must sometimes seem," he declared, "reducing every question to the Communist equation. Some of the questions are bigger than communism. . . . *If all the Communists on earth disappeared overnight, the need for foreign aid to assist new struggling peoples to achieve stable democratic societies would still be there.*" He and Nehru were completely on the same wavelength in this regard (Bowles 1951).

The tragedy is that events were destined to overtake this potentially promising opening, which Ambassador Bowles's remarkable sensitivity to emerging attitudes in the crystallizing Third World revealed. He was already being politically beleaguered at home by the hard-line faction that was moving to the forefront of the Truman administration and was gaining momentum as well in the rival Republican Party, which saw in the mounting anticommunist hysteria that the postwar rivalry between the United States, on the one hand, and the Soviet Union and Maoist China, on the other, was spawning, an opportunity to return to power after a sixteen-year hiatus.

Chester Bowles's activist style of diplomacy, along with his opposition to the rapidly crystallizing conventional wisdom about how best to checkmate Soviet expansionism, made him a highly controversial emissary. One might say that in Indian eyes he made U.S. South Asian foreign policy appear to be more progressive than actually it was. Neither the Truman administration nor the U.S. Congress were particularly enthusiastic about Nehru's Fabian approach to Indian economic development nor his reluctance to decisively lead his nation into the Western camp. The so-called "non-alignment doctrine" was interpreted as being equivalent in the international arena to what the term "fellow traveler" connoted in the McCarthyist atmosphere that was pervading the domestic American political environment. It was mainly Bowles's unremitting assertion that India constituted no threat to American strategic interests as long as she remained democratic, non-aligned, and at peace with her neighbors that helped keep the hardliners at bay for the remainder of Truman's tenure in office.

Bowles's achievement was quite remarkable in the face of the pattern of strategic thinking, which already pervaded the State and Defense departments. Secretary of State Dean Acheson passionately believed that countervailing military power could alone successfully contain communist expansionism. Men like James C. Forrestal (Secretary of the Navy) and Clark Clifford (a perennial advisor to American presidents) were if anything even more adamant about this than was Acheson (see Acheson 1969). Along with their influence on President Truman, was the impact which White Hall and men like Sir Olaf Caroe were having on the debate taking place within the foreign policy community as America groped for a strategic doctrine suited to the perceived requirements of an emergent, self-proclaimed superpower (Caroe 1958).

The national elections in 1952, which brought to power the Republican Party and General Dwight D. Eisenhower, would prove to be the decisive turning point, which would set the course for U.S. South Asia policy for the next half century. This was the fatal decision to militarize that policy and incorporate South Asia into the nexus of the Cold War via arms aid to Pakistan. In personal terms, it conclusively replaced the creative pragmatism embodied by Ambassador Chester Bowles with the doctrinaire anticommunism of Secretary of State John Foster Dulles.

3

THE EISENHOWER ADMINISTRATION (1953–1961)

Clearly, the lynchpin of the Eisenhower Administration from the standpoint of South Asia policy was the imprint, which Secretary of State John Foster Dulles and his hawkish supporters etched on it (see Mosley 1978).[1] With Chester Bowles and the New Dealers consigned to political limbo following the Republicans' electoral triumph in 1952, and the descent of the American public into a frenzy of anticommunist witch-hunting under the impact of "McCarthyism," few political obstacles remained in Mr Dulles's way. He was free to incorporate Pakistan into the network of militarized client states with which he proposed to encircle the communist world. For, prior to Dulles's ascent after the Eisenhower administration took office, it had been not only Chester Bowles who questioned the veracity of this policy; even more conservative Democrats like Secretary of State Dean Acheson himself had his doubts about it, despite his otherwise strong support for the containment doctrine. His attitude toward Pakistan's willingness to help in the defense of the Middle East remained one of wariness, "lest arming Pakistan ensnare the United States in India–Pakistan disputes" (Acheson 1950: 138). Chief of Staff, General Omar Bradley, opined, "If we give Pakistan military aid we will find ourselves in trouble with India"(Kux 2001: 47).

As is well known, John Foster Dulles emerged as the country's new foreign policy apostle. The word apostle is highly apt. It was not only the fact that Dulles represented a radical departure from the global perspectives of the bulk of his immediate Democratic predecessors. His real achievement was his ability to infuse American foreign policy with an ideological intensity that was the equal of and opposite to the edge that Marxist-Leninist ideology had imparted to Soviet (and later Chinese) foreign policy. Extremism had bred counter extremism. The British philosopher, Bertand Russell, characterized men like Dulles on the Western Side and Stalin and Kruschchev on the Soviet side as "rival fanatics."

Predictably and understandably, therefore, once John Foster Dulles became Secretary of State, U.S. policy toward South Asia pointedly turned away from an emphasis on the patient nurturance of democratic institutions and economic development for which Chester Bowles and other New Dealers had stood. In its place came a policy that denied legitimacy to India's non-alignment doctrine, because it was not stridently anticommunist, as Dulles would have it, and blatantly recruited Pakistan into the mosaic of containment alliances that were already falling in place along the perimeter of Soviet and Chinese power. Pakistan became America's strategic counterfoil in South Asia, both against the communist bloc, because of its expansionism, and India, because of its "neutralism." At one point, Dulles had publicly denounced Nehru's "neutralism" as "immoral." The foundation for the disconnect between militarized grand strategy and a sensible, historically enlightened pragmatism that would lead to American diplomatic failure in South Asia was laid.

Pakistan readily joined the Grand Alliance, not because it faced credible threats either from internal communist subversion or external communist aggression, but solely because its leaders perceived this as a necessary way to equalize the imagined power gap *vis-à-vis* India. Having already unsuccessfully waged war against India over Kashmir in 1948, alliance with the United States, it was reasoned, would enable Pakistan to "double-dip," as it were, on American military and economic resources in order to create a military machine capable of eventually waging a war of revenge against India. "The United States was Pakistan's great power of choice," declares Husain Haqqani. "Alliance with the United States became as important a part of the plans for consolidating the Pakistani nation and state as Islam and opposition to Hindu India . . . Pakistan's intelligence community fabricated evidence of a communist threat to Pakistan to get the U.S.' attention" (Haqqani 2005: 32).

Lack of regional sophistication and historical depth lay behind the Eisenhower administration's inability to perceive these crucial nuances. Eurocentric anticommunist ideologues like John Foster Dulles and his supporters saw the world almost entirely in one-dimensional terms; not unlike the NeoCons who until recently dominated American foreign policy. The absence of adequate regional expertise denied them any opportunity to be made aware of the fact that the principal regional threat in South Asia was not communism (either internal or external) but a contemporary manifestation of a centuries old pattern of ethno-religious enmity (Gallagher et al. 1973; Gould 1994; Robinson 1974; Seal 1968).[2]

The appalling depths of Mr Dulles's ignorance of the South Asia region was vividly displayed during a dinner-party conversation, which the Secretary had with the famous journalist, Walter Lippman, shortly after the 1954 Geneva Accords. "Look Walter," Dulles said, blinking behind his thick glasses, "I've got some real fighting men into the south of Asia. The only Asians who can really fight are the Pakistanis. That's why we need them in the alliance. We could never get along without the Gurkhas." When Lippman reminded him that the Gurkhas are Indian, not Pakistani, Dulles replied, "Well, they may not be Pakistanis, but they're Moslems." Lippman once more corrected Dulles, saying, "No, I'm afraid they're not Moslems either, they're Hindus." Dulles merely replied, "No matter," and proceeded to lecture Lippman for half an hour on how *SEATO* would plug the dike against communism in Asia (Barnet 1983: 34).[3]

The wheels began falling off the Pakistan policy almost as soon as it commenced. The trouble was that, "the United States and Pakistan entered the alliance for different and ultimately conflicting reasons." While anti-communist in ideological orientation, says Kux, "Pakistan remained at heart concerned about the threat from India rather than any menace from the communists" (Kux 2001: 84).

America's relationship with its new ally steadily sank into a political quagmire. It soon became evident that the difference between global and regional orientations had resulted in a vast chasm between what Pakistan and the United States expected of each other. Once this became obvious, President Eisenhower himself grew disillusioned with the policy. At a National Security Council Meeting the President said he felt that "our tendency to rush out and seek allies was not very sensible." He voiced concern that "we [are] doing practically nothing for Pakistan except in the form of military aid." The military commitment to Pakistan was "perhaps the worst kind of a plan and decision we could have made," Eisenhower lamented. "It was a terrible error, but we now seem hopelessly involved in it" (see McMahon 1994: 207). He attempted to ameliorate Dulles's hard line by reaching out to Nehru, even to the point of inviting Nehru to Washington in 1956 and then visiting India in 1959. The two leaders hit it off well.

Photograph 3.1: U.S. President Dwight D. Eisenhower welcomes Indian Prime Minister Jawaharlal Nehru to the White House in Washington in 1956

Photograph 3.2: During the 1956 state visit of Prime Minister Jawaharlal Nehru to the U.S. with U.S. President Dwight D. Eisenhower

But unfortunately Eisenhower was unwilling to completely abandon the Pakistan alliance. This left Nehru no alternative in the face of the steady militarization of Pakistan but to edge closer to the Soviet Union in strategic terms in order to offset American support for Pakistan.

What this meant is that the cardinal ingredient of the Cold War-driven U.S. strategic orientation to South Asia had failed by the end of the Eisenhower administration. The Soviet Union had "penetrated" the region and was in a position to influence the outcome of events there.

Photograph 3.3: President Eisenhower with Indian President Dr Rajendra Prasad during U.S. President's visit to India in December 1959

India had been driven into the arms of the communist bloc; not totally, of course; not in terms of grass-roots revolution or regime change; but in the sense that the Soviets now enjoyed a measure strategic leverage in the region; something which the ayatollahs of Cold War theology believed they could prevent by arming Pakistan and checkmating neutralist India. Their policy had the opposite effect.

Photograph 3.4: A beaming President Eisenhower addresses Delhi's citizens in December 1959

Photograph 3.5: President Eisenhower and Pakistan's President Mohammad Ayub Khan watch a horsemanship display by lancers by the mounted guard on polo field near Presidential Palace in Karachi, December 8, 1959. Pakistan is the third stop on Ike's 11-nation tour

4

THE KENNEDY ADMINISTRATION (1961–1963)

John F. Kennedy's personal impact on U.S.–Indian relations was short lived because his own life was cut short by an assassin's bullets on November 22, 1963. His tenure, however, while plagued with numerous competing challenges, did last long enough for his administration to considerably amplify the new tone set by President Eisenhower during his second term, and to initiate some policy modifications that moved toward a more amicable and balanced approach to South Asia which, of course, proved upsetting to Pakistan.

As noted, Eisenhower actually had begun this process during his second term in order to soften his Secretary of State's strident "moralistic politics," which, in the words of Arthur M. Schlesinger, Jr., saw "the world as irrevocably split into two unified and hostile blocs" (Schlesinger 1967: 428). India and Nehru clearly did not fit into this crude dichotomy and therein lay the obstacle, which inhibited constructive relations between the two countries. Kennedy carried the change forward and tried to constructively elaborate on it. The end result was essentially a "dual models" approach to South Asia, which stressed major increases in economic aid for India and greater respect for her non-alignment doctrine, while continuing to stress military assistance to Pakistan in recognition of her membership in *SEATO* and *CENTO*. The flaw, of course, from India's standpoint and from the standpoint of intra-regional stability, was indeed that the military relationship with Pakistan remained in effect.

The "dual models" strategy had another, extra-regional dimension as well. This arose from the Soviet Union's decision after Stalin to revert to the old Leninist policy of cultivating the "bourgeois" ruling classes in Third World countries by accepting their legitimacy, toning down orthodox revolutionary Marxist-Leninist rhetoric, and promoting economic assistance, diplomatic succor, and "friendship" among them. This was an implicit differentiation between Western and non-Western ruling elites with a view to recruiting the latter into the Socialist camp on the basis of "anti-colonialism." Economic aid, in this context, became a crucial weapon in the Cold War—

that is, which side could offer the most material blandishments. By stressing economic aid to India, and endorsing the development of her democratic institutions as *prima facie* deterrents to the spread of totalitarian communism, the Kennedy administration systematized this approach, and to that extent actually returned to the essence of Chester Bowles's original thesis—*viz.*, juxtaposing "security" with "development," "secularism," and "democracy."

To personalize his commitment, he appointed Harvard professor John Kenneth Galbraith (1909–2006) as U.S. ambassador in 1961 (see Galbraith 1969). A noted scholar, an intellectual and social philosopher in his own right, and a dedicated liberal, Galbraith had the right credentials for achieving rapport with India's contemplative, at times Prince Hamlet-like, prime minister.

Ironically, the China War in 1962 for a time materially abetted the rapprochement process. India's dire military straits tempted Nehru to move away from non-alignment and communist bloc *bhai-bhai* toward a strategic relationship with the United States when Chinese forces burst into *NEFA* and appeared poised to overrun all of eastern India. But when the Chinese suddenly aborted their incursion and settled for an "object lesson" in Maoist political self-righteousness, Nehru, to the consternation of Washington, returned India to its orthodox non-aligned posture and resumed his criticism of the military model from which he had just so munificently benefitted.[1]

Once set in motion, and despite the China War interlude, the dualistic model did acquire some saliency in South Asia, but only up to a point. Along with the aforementioned continuing strategic relationship with Pakistan, Kennedy had many other matters on his mind. There was the Bay of Pigs fiasco followed by the Cuban Missile Crisis, which occurred about the same time as the China War. The Vietnam imbroglio, whose origins he had inherited from the French, and the Eisenhower administration was heating up and the President found himself compelled to devote more and more of his time to its increasingly arcane permutations.

Then there was President Kennedy's relationship with Nehru, which failed ever to achieve the kind of personal rapport which might have been expected, given the fact that Kennedy had publicly expressed his admiration for Nehru's "soaring idealism," and had called for "more cooperative relations with the 'uncommitted world.'" Then when they met face to face in Washington in 1961, their encounter did not go well. Kennedy already had some negative feelings because when earlier he visited India as a young congressman, Nehru had high-browed him. Furthermore, Nehru's tendency towards "international self-righteousness" led Kennedy to view him "as almost the John Foster Dulles of neutralism" (Schlesinger 1967: 417). By the time Nehru reached

Washington he was in his seventies and clearly showing his age, and Kennedy found him to be "terribly passive." Kennedy said that it was "like trying to grab something in your hand, only to have it turn out just to be fog." It was, said Kennedy, "a disaster . . . the worst head-of-state visit I have had" (Schlesinger 1967: 420).

Photograph 4.1: President John F. Kennedy and Indian Prime Minister Jawaharlal Nehru during the latter's third and final visit to the U.S. in November 1961

Nevertheless, the Kennedy administration pressed ahead with as much reform of the U.S.–Indian relationship as they felt was realistically possible under existing international conditions, and in the face of the intra-regional constraints imposed by the Pakistan alliance.

General Ayub Khan, after bringing in military dictator-ship to Pakistan by 1959, had arrived in Washington on the heels of Nehru in the Fall of 1962. He came to try and undo or at least equalize any concessions Kennedy might have made to India regarding economic aid, military assistance (in the light of the Chinese attack), or the Kashmir dispute (see Galbraith 1969; Kux 1993, 2001). Vice-President Lyndon Johnson was sent off to India and Pakistan to placate the doubters and critics in both countries. Johnson's naivete about international affairs and his historical ignorance about South Asia transformed his sortie into a public relations spectacle that was essentially meaningless. Informants of mine who accompanied Johnson said that he behaved like a Texas politician running for office in the United States. He would spot a group of spectators by the side of the road, enter their midst, and give a speech, which his translators laughingly would render into Hindi or Urdu in phrases that bore no relationship at all to what he had said in English!

There was, however, one respect in which Johnson's South Asian tour was less than farcical and would have profound implications for the next phase in U.S. South Asian diplomacy: It was the personal rapport that developed between Lyndon Johnson and Ayub Khan. This inclined the vice-president to adopt a strong stance in favor of the Pakistan alliance at the very point where President Kennedy was inclining in the opposite

Photograph 4.2: Dr Sarvepalli Radhakrishnan, President of India, greeted with a parade given in his honor by President Kennedy

direction. Despite the personal difficulties with Nehru, the president decided that not only should economic aid to India be substantially increased but that a more meaningful military relationship between the two countries must be developed as well. An agreement to this effect had been prepared for Kennedy's signature, but never was consummated due to his assassination on November 23, 1963. Symbolic of this contemplated closer relationship was the return of Chester Bowles as Ambassador on July 17, 1963 (see Kux 1993; Schaffer 1993). President Johnson, due to his partisanship toward Ayub's Pakistan, was uninclined to implement this agreement.

5

THE JOHNSON ADMINISTRATION (1963–1969)

President John F. Kennedy's funeral occurred on November 25, 1963. His death heralded another character change in U.S. administrations, without a change of parties. John F. Kennedy was a sophisticated intellectual with a good feel for things international. He was "to the manner born," so to speak; the scion of an elite Irish–American family that had risen far above their immigrant roots to take their place as members of the so-called "East Coast Establishment." His father had been Ambassador to England; he was the author of a Pulitzer Prize-winning book (*Profiles in Courage*) (Kennedy 1956).

Lyndon Baines Johnson, by contrast, was a rough-hewn, grass-roots Texas politician with a small-college education; he was a master of political hardball but virtually devoid of any international experience or expertise (see Goodwin 1976/1991: 160–169). With little in common intellectually or socially, their presence together on the Democratic Party ticket of 1960 had been a matter of pure political expediency.

The differences between these two men, in the context of Kennedy's death, and Johnson's accession to the presidency, bore resemblances to Harry Truman's situation following Roosevelt's demise. Like Truman, his limited international experience and homespun political instincts would make it difficult for him to cope with the complexities and nuances of world politics. In the case of South Asia, Johnson overtly subscribed to the "dual models" doctrine that President Kennedy was endeavoring to promulgate, but, as suggested, not without reservations. "The new president was . . . unsympathetic to his predecessor's desire to shift the policy from Pakistan to India" (Kux 2001: 148). However, his confidence, even about this, eroded considerably once he was compelled to deal in a hands-on fashion with the wiles and complexities of Ayub Khan and Zulfikar Ali Bhutto, the death of Jawaharlal Nehru on May 27, 1964, and the ensuing leadership crisis in India, which ultimately led to the rise of Indira Gandhi, the outbreak of war between India and Pakistan on May 13, 1965, drought and near-famine in the eastern Gangetic plain in 1966–67, and the United States's mounting involvement in the Vietnam quagmire.

The Pakistan conundrum provided his initial baptism of fire, and the first indications that he might be in over his head. During his vice-presidency he had been thoroughly taken in by Ayub Khan's "Colonel Blimp," "can-do" personality, and entered his presidency with expectations that here was a man with whom he would be able to enjoy a working relationship. He soon learned otherwise, but also learned that dealing with the Indian leadership would be no picnic either. There were deep historical antipathies between India and Pakistan, which could not be papered over with glittering generalities. The impact of this dawning political reality was to make him wary, petulant, and at times vindictive about the political obstacles he encountered in South Asia, particularly after U.S. troubles in Vietnam entered the mix.

Things came to a head with Pakistan soon after Johnson became president. Bhutto's star was on the rise in Islamabad; he was increasingly asserting a distinct, maverick political identity, which increasingly challenged Ayub's exclusive suzerainty; he was a stormy petrel whose Pakistan People's Party (PPP), demanded more democracy at home, and greater flexibility in Pakistani foreign policy. This included cultivating relations with China as a counterfoil to the almost pathological threat that both he and Ayub believed India represented. Johnson was insufficiently attuned to the fact that this paranoia actually stemmed from the Muslim Separatist Movement whose history reached back to the turn of the century and had been the impetus for the creation of Pakistan in the first place. In the face of these kinds of domestic pressures, Ayub's patently irrational demands that the United States incorporate in the Alliance guarantees against Indian "aggression," combined with Bhutto's playing up to China, finally got under Johnson's skin. There was an encounter between Bhutto and Johnson in the Oval Office at the time of the Kennedy's funeral (which Ayub did not attend due to pique over Kennedy's tilt toward India); it got so testy that the President "brusquely told him to sit down and launched into animated discussion of U.S.–Pakistani differences" (Kux 2001: 148). Johnson had come a distance from the point as vice-president when he had asked a staffer, "Why is it that Jack Kennedy and you India lovers in the State Department are so Goddamned ornery to my friend Ayub" (ibid.).

A comparable evolution occurred with respect to Johnson's relationship with Indira Gandhi after her ascent to prime ministership in 1966. Her visit to Washington two months after she assumed office went surprisingly well. Mrs Gandhi charmed an American President who was notably responsive to being charmed, especially by women. As one American official put it,

"She set out to vamp LBJ and succeeded" (Kux 1993:
250). Her principal motive at the time was to ameliorate
Johnson's "short tether" food policy, which had been
sold to him by Secretary Orville Freeman and other
puritanical agricultural experts who held that India was
profligately importing PL480 food grains as a substitute
for stimulating its own food-growing capabilities, in
order to free domestic capital for industrialization, which
both Nehru and his daughter believed to be the magic
key to liberating India from postcolonial paternalism.[1]
The only trouble was that Johnson's sanctimoniousness
had come in the midst of the Bihar famine! Mrs Gandhi
remarked to an Indian reporter that "my mission is
to get food and foreign exchange without appearing
to ask for them" (ibid.). Ambassador Bowles was
opposed to "short tether" and tried to thwart its imple-
mentation in the face of a November 1966 "bipartisan"
joint-Congressional delegation consisting of Congress-
men Poage and (and later, Senator) Dole and Senators
Miller and McGee, which Johnson had sent out to
India to provide legitimation for the new policy. One
informant characterized the mission's precooked report
as "Johnson's 'Gulf of Tonkin Resolution' for India."[2]

This maneuver, along with the rupee devaluation,
which many of her critics believed a naive Mrs Gandhi
had been hoodwinked into agreeing to by American free-
marketeers, ended the brief honeymoon between the
two leaders. Mrs Gandhi was compelled to fight for her

political life and did so by abruptly turning to the Left and adopting a more populist political posture at home, renewed rapprochement with the Soviets, and more pointed criticism of U.S.–Vietnam policy. She was helped by the fact that the Green Revolution was kicking in and making India less dependent on U.S. grain shipments.

By the end of Lyndon Johnson's tenure, U.S.–Indian relations had cooled considerably and the perception of India by the American political establishment as a "soft state" had taken root. U.S.–Pakistan relations had turned increasingly sour as well once it had become clear to the Pakistanis in the aftermath of the 1965 war that their American "ally" was not prepared to issue a blank check in support of their thirst for political revenge against hated India. And in any event, the Johnson administration was now mired completely in the Vietnam misadventure.

6

THE NIXON ADMINISTRATION (1969–1974)

After Richard M. Nixon lost the presidential election to John F. Kennedy in 1960, he returned to California, ran for the position of the governor of that state, and lost once again. Completely out of office, he set about to rehabilitate his political image. One of the methods he employed was to make a global tour in order to re-establish his *bona fides* as an authority on international relations. His itinerary included stops in South Asia. He first visited India and then Pakistan. In the words of former Senator Charles F. Percy of Illinois (personal interview), "the Nehrus treated him not only like a defeated governor of California, but also like one who had lost an election for dog catcher!"

When he moved on to Pakistan, however, Field Marshal Ayub Khan rolled out the red carpet for him and treated him like visiting royalty. This difference in receptions made a lasting impression on Richard Nixon, which drove his orientation to South Asia throughout his presidency.

It is fair to say that the Nixon administration marked the nadir of U.S.–Indian relations, at least since John Foster Dulles's heyday in the first Eisenhower administration when, significantly, Nixon was the vice-president. Nixon made no secret of the fact, at least in private, that he detested the Nehrus and wanted to do his utmost to discredit and politically isolate and punish India. Currying Pakistan was his weapon of choice for achieving this end. Unfolding events in the Subcontinent provided much fuel for Nixon's pursuit of enmity.

Commencing in 1969, Nixon's animus against India drove him to fully revitalize the militarized grand strategy of the Dulles era. These developments dramatized once again the chronic, fallacious American belief that any strategic model, which either by default or design essentially pitted Pakistan against India could be a successful basis for effectively managing U.S. interests in the Subcontinent.

The Bangladesh War in 1971 was a further testament to the futility of this counterproductive orientation to the region. The circumstances which led to it, and the U.S. role in tacitly siding with Pakistan, especially after war erupted between the two South Asian states, marked the point where India, under Indira Gandhi, decided to counter Nixonian hubris through establishing a more explicit strategic relationship with the Soviet Union, and the assertion of her determination to make India the hegemonic power in South Asia.

Photograph 6.1: Indian Prime Minister Indira Gandhi with Mrs Martin Luther King Jr. and Walter Fauntroy, U.S. Representative of the District of Columbia, at Blair House in Washington on November 5, 1971

From the American standpoint, therefore, Bangladesh was more than another outgrowth of the flawed policies of the past. It must be adjudged a rather shallow, amateurish attempt to pursue a pattern of power politics that virtually destroyed what was left of American prestige and credibility in the Subcontinent. So shallow and crude it was, as a matter of fact, that it cast considerable doubt on the reputation for shrewdness and strategic perspicacity that mainstream foreign policy commentators often attributed, and even now attributes, to Richard Nixon and Henry Kissinger.

When Pakistan's next military dictator, general Yahya Khan, turned his country's American-equipped army against his own people, on March 26, in a brutal but unsuccessful attempt to suppress secession in East Pakistan, the U.S. government acted even more than it had in the past as an enabler of political repression where the obvious choice was between supporting democracy or legitimizing dictatorship.

The record clearly shows that the principal motivation for the famous "tilt" toward Pakistan after war broke out between India and Pakistan over Bangladesh were (*i*) Nixon's irrational animosity toward India, and (*ii*) his and Kissinger's determination to let nothing, even genocide, stand in the way of facilitating the president's impending "opening" to China.

As is well known, Kissinger had made his secret journey to Beijing on July 10, 1971, via Pakistan to prepare the ground for the President's visit. Now, he and Nixon were fearful that war between India and Pakistan would somehow disrupt the scenario for the President's impending trip. When war did break out, there was pique and exasperation, almost an attitude of, "How could they do this to us at such a crucial moment?" While Nixon paid lip-service to the "intrinsic tragedy" that was unfolding, he privately lamented that it "could disrupt . . . our policy toward China" (Kux 2001: 194). Wanting to placate Yahya in order to keep him in the China game, Christopher Hitchens says, "In late April 1971, at the very height of the mass murder, Kissinger sent a message to General Yahya Khan, *thanking him for his* 'delicacy and tact' " (emphasis added). He also declares that, "The Kissinger policy towards Bangladesh may well have been largely conducted for its own sake as a means of gratifying his boss's animus against India" (Hitchens 2001: 46–47). As already noted, personal animus obviously did play a role in fanning Nixon's hysterical assertions that India intended to use the Bangladesh war as an excuse to dismember Pakistan. However, the saber-rattling to which he resorted, particularly the touch of gunboat diplomacy when a carrier task force sailed up the Bay of Bengal, also had a larger purpose. As Kissinger puts it in his memoirs: While indeed the "unstated mission of the Enterprise, never spelled out to the U.S. Navy, was to send a signal to the Indians and the Soviets to give emphasis to our warnings about West Pakistan," it was also undertaken as a ploy to impress the Chinese that "if they entered into a relationship with the United States they could count on US steadfastness in times of trouble" (Kissinger 1979: 305). This sophomoric diplomacy, however, must not be seen exclusively in terms of the venality and pettiness of an individual American President and his macho Secretary of State. It must as well be seen as one more manifestation of a bankrupt foreign policy that repeatedly undermined its own declared premises.

The new balance of forces that ensued quickly fell into place. Indira visited Moscow in September 1971 after having signed a friendship treaty with the USSR in August. Although not a formal alliance, it nevertheless "provided for bilateral consultations in the event of crises and pledged that neither country would support a third party against the other." Most important, the new relationship provided "the full support and additional military supplies for which the Indians had been pressing" (Kux 1993: 195). Next, India exploded a nuclear device on May 8, 1974, signaling thereby an intensification of India's determination to become a major regional power and see to her own security. Finally, she retaliated against "short Tether" diplomacy by renouncing further dependence on American economic assistance (Bjorkmanm 1980; Ganguly 1992; Gould 1990).

The Vietnam and Bangladesh wars, the opening to China, and the crude resort to economic coercion and political blackmail had thus administered the *coup de grâce* to what remained of the original American strategic scenario for South Asia. The policies subsequently pursued by the Carter (1977–1981), Reagan–Bush (1981–1993), Clinton (1993–2001), and Bush-2 (2001–2009) administrations all reflected this structural change in one way or another, as we shall see.

7

THE FORD ADMINISTRATION (1974–1977)

The recently deceased Gerald Ford succeeded the disgraced Richard Nixon as the 38th president of the United States on August 9, 1974. He retained Henry Kissinger as his Secretary of State despite the controversial role he had played in the Vietnam disaster, the Bangladesh war, and finally the disintegration of the Nixon administration. This meant that the dismissive attitude, which Kissinger and his recent boss harbored toward India remained in place for the time being. When former Attorney General William Saxbe, was appointed Ambassador Extraordinary and Plenipotentiary to India in 1975, he paid the customary courtesy call on the Secretary of State prior to his departure to New Delhi. Kissinger's last words to him were, "Once you reach India, I don't want to hear from you again!" (personal interview).

By the time President Ford took office, many new challenges had arisen in South Asia that were byproducts of past American policy failures, both in Pakistan and India. First and foremost, of course, was the fact that India by then had surreptitiously acquired a nuclear arsenal and Pakistan would soon follow with one of its own.

In Pakistan, the ascent of Zulfikar Ali Bhutto was especially troublesome. While paying lip-service to American support in the recently concluded Bangladesh War, Bhutto in fact, set out to severely attenuate Pakistan's participation in the American global security system. Before he was finally done-in by the combination of his personal political pathologies and the machinations of the country's disgruntled antidemocratic elites, Bhutto, on the positive side, had moved Pakistan closer to the achievement of genuine popular government than at any time in its history. On the negative side, from the standpoint of American interests, Bhutto had proceeded to abandon *SEATO* and *CENTO*, had established links to the non-aligned movement, had developed a relationship with China that was structurally equivalent to India's counterfoil relationship with the Soviet Union, had opened up a relationship with North Korea (thereby laying the foundations for the eventual development of a

Pakistani nuclear bomb, and A.Q. Khan's machinations), had established lucrative economic ties with the Gulf states, which reduced Pakistani dependence on American aid, and made Pakistan an active player in the *Organization of the Islamic Conference (OIC)* (Burki 1980).

As had been the case with previous milestones in U.S.–Indian relations, some measure of de-escalation in tone was attempted toward the end of the Nixon administration. A crucial gesture was the appointment of Daniel Patrick Moynihan to replace former Senator Kenneth Keating as Ambassador. Like Ambassador George Allen after Dulles initiated the Pakistan alliance, Keating inherited the political fallout that followed the Nixon-Kissinger "tilt." Moynihan, like Galbraith, was an eminent scholar whom both the Indian intellectual and political establishments respected, even though he was not as politically liberal as his relevant counterparts—*viz.*, Bowles and Galbraith. According to Thomas Thornton, Moynihan rather paternalistically defined his mission to India as waiting "until the Indians were prepared to settle for a more traditional relationship of diplomacy rather than tutelage" (Thornton 1992: 106).

As a follow-up, and not unlike Dulles in an earlier time, Kissinger also made a pilgrimage to India (October 27–30, 1974) at the outset of the Ford administration to try to mend some fences. In Thornton's words, "Kissinger . . . intended to use it as a major signal to the Indians of the seriousness of the new policy approach"

(Thornton 1992: 110). While Kissinger "saw his presence to be a boon to be granted to favored nations ... as a sign that the host country 'mattered,'" Mrs Gandhi clearly saw it otherwise in as much as she managed to be on tour in Kashmir during the Secretary of State's visit (Kux 1993: 328)!

The two most important issues that affected the relationship during President Ford's brief tenure were the 1974 nuclear tests and Mrs Gandhi's suspension of democracy in June 1975—the so-called Emergency. The dictatorship endured for two years and resulted in much oppression and suffering for many members of the political opposition. Jayaprakash Narain, the embodiment of the "JP Movement," which brought Mrs Gandhi down and prompted her to declare the Emergency that terminated parliamentary democracy for the first and only time in post-Independence Indian history, was held incommunicado for months at a time when he was in delicate health. It was, however, a badly managed dictatorship, out of accord with the Indian political temperament. By 1977, Mrs Gandhi terminated it and declared new elections in which she and the Congress Party were resoundingly defeated, leading to the Janata government and Morarji Desai's accession to the prime-ministership. International pressure, especially emanating from the pro-Indian sector of the American liberal establishment, apparently played a major behind-the-scenes role in Mrs Gandhi's decision to restore democracy. Senator Charles Percy was a close personal friend of Mrs Gandhi who had a private visit with her during this period. "I told her," he said, "that as long as you continue this Emergency your American friends will completely withhold support for India." This conversation occurred shortly before the Emergency was ended, and Percy believed it played a significant role in her decision (personal interview with the author).

The other issue, of course, was nuclear proliferation. The Ford administration would commence a process that would ramify widely through all subsequent administrations in their dealings with India and South Asia. What had made the nuclear issue especially testy was the fact that the agreement the countries signed in 1963 for building and refueling the two reactors at Tarapur included an understanding that India would refrain from weaponizing its nuclear capability. When India exploded its "nuclear device" in 1974, there were strong recriminations in the United States and the West generally. Surprisingly, however, Secretary Kissinger decided to play it cool. "Kissinger overruled his advisers and passed word through the government that there would be no inflammatory rhetoric . . . nor punitive measures . . . undertaken" (Thornton 1992: 112). This seems to have fitted into Kissinger's preference for "reality-based" diplomacy over "moral politics." He took that same attitude toward the Emergency. His reasoning in both cases was that blatant recriminations would impel India to move closer to the Soviet Union than it already had. Moynihan's successor, the "exiled" ambassador Saxbe reinforced this perspective during his tenure. He took the view that America was far more important to India than *vice versa* and that the United States could afford to wait and see what sort of relationship India wished to have.[1]

Either because of or despite this orientation, perhaps a bit of both, Indira did seem to come around to some degree, apparently because she felt that India had moved too far toward the Soviet Union, so much so that it was strengthening the coercive powers of the pro-Soviet faction within her Congress coalition at the cost of jeopardizing her latitude for maneuver in the domestic political arena. All this set the stage for the processes that came into play with the ensuing Carter administration.

8

THE CARTER ADMINISTRATION (1977–1981)

J immy Carter, both because of his personal values and the evolving strategic situation in South Asia, was the first to systematically undertake an adaptive orientation to the proliferation challenge. He did indeed endeavor to depart from Kissingeresque real politik and initiate a genre of moral politics, which until the Soviet invasion of Afghanistan focused almost exclusively on nuclear proliferation—that is, attempting to manage the consequences of Pakistan's and India's newly asserted determination to establish and enhance their nuclear sinews and chart their own political course independent of American tutelage. Economic aid, once conceived to be the magic key for enticing India into the American camp, was now downgraded to a policy of "meeting basic needs." In Tahir-Kheli's words, "The Carter administration elevated nonproliferation to the forefront of American foreign policy concerns." This initiative was given a self-serving spin by conceptualizing it as an aspect of what was called the "Carter-Brzezinski policy." According to Robert Goheen, who was Carter's ambassador to India, its stated purpose was to "cultivate regionally influential countries as a means of devolving some of the excessive responsibilities [*sic*] that the United States had assumed in the post-War decades." The term "excessive" has a martyrish ring to it; but the implication was clearly that the Carter administration wanted to fashion a multinational forum of some kind for addressing proliferation in South Asia. It did not want to bear all the burdens alone (Goheen 1992: 122).

Goheen saw this early phase of the Carter administration in an essentially positive light, despite tensions over the supply of enriched uranium for the Tarapur nuclear reactor. He felt that the Simla agreement negotiated between Zulfikar Ali Bhutto and Mrs Gandhi had resolved many perplexing issues and markedly reduced tensions between India and Pakistan. He felt that a balance had been struck in the United States's relations with the two South Asian states, which embodied the kind of limited-interventionist, two-track bilateralism, that the administration henceforth wished to pursue.

When Morarji Desai assumed office as Prime Minister under Janata Party rule (1977–1979), the United States found they had an Indian politician who was ideally suited to the new dispensation. Desai was far more centrist and pledged to pursue a more even-handed non-alignment policy than his predecessors.

However, the honeymoon was not destined to last very long. As the Carter administration neared the end of its tenure, three disruptive events disturbed the relative political tranquility. Unfortunately, the Soviet invasion of Afghanistan on December 19, 1979, Mrs Gandhi's return to power in January,1980, plus the

Photograph 8.1: U.S. President Jimmy Carter and his wife's visit to New Delhi on January 1, 1978

Photograph 8.2: Indian Prime Minister Morarji Desai and U.S. President Jimmy Carter sign the Delhi Declaration

U.S. Senate's refusal to approve the second shipment of enriched uranium for Tarapur, all intruded once again and muddied the diplomatic waters.

When the Soviets struck in Afghanistan, the ensuing crisis elicited an immediate knee-jerk reaction in the White House and on Capitol Hill. Pakistan almost at once regained her image as a "frontline state" in the struggle to block any further southerly extensions of Soviet influence and power. Representatives of the Carter administration fanned out in South Asia to sell their new containment policy. National Security Advisor Sbigniew Brzezinski and Secretary of State Warren Christopher visited Pakistan, whose president was the country's latest military dictator, Zia-ul-Haq, to try and reinstate some semblance of the old Cold War alliance. Simultaneously, another team headed for New Delhi to seek Indian acquiescence

Photograph 8.3: Pakistan's President Gen. Mohammed Zia-ul-Haq (left) and his guest former U.S. President Jimmy Carter listen, Monday, November 3, 1986 in Peshawar, to Afghan refugee leaders during a meeting at a refugee camp near Peshawar. Carter and his wife visited several parts of the sprawling camp

in their plan to once again reinvigorate the Pakistani military machine as a counterfoil to Soviet aggression. In Islamabad, Brzezinski and Christopher offered Pakistan USD 400 million worth of "immediate assistance" as an inducement to strengthen their frontier forces. General Zia sniffed at this, calling it "peanuts," because he knew the United States was over a barrel and rightly saw it as an opportunity to resuscitate the old policy model from which the Pakistani elite had so handsomely profited throughout the Cold War. Presidential advisor Clark Clifford and State Department Representative Howard Schaffer arrived in New Delhi on the same day that their counterparts reached Islamabad to try and convince the newly installed Indira Gandhi government that the Soviet invasion of Afghanistan represented as much a threat to India as to Pakistan. While then External Affairs Minister, P.V. Narasimha Rao, agreed that the Soviet action constituted a serious problem for the region, he rejected the proposed U.S. solution. Remembering the result of past attempts to arm Pakistan as a buffer against external threats, he retorted that India's preference was for measures that prevented any further introduction of arms into the Subcontinent by all parties (personal interview). It was in some ways the equal and opposite reaction to Pakistan's when, during the China War, India sought American military assistance. Invariably it comes down to perceived interests!

For a time, therefore, the invasion of Afghanistan had reawakened the "Pakistan lobby" in Washington, and had correspondingly aroused expectations in Pakistan itself that a renewed militarized grand strategy would, as had been the case at the height of the Cold War, prove to be a boon to the country's antidemocratic elites. Husain Haqqani has characterized Pakistan under its military rulers and their civilian cohorts as a "rent-seeking state, living off the rents of its strategic location," a state of affairs that has existed "since its involvement in U.S.-sponsored treaties of the cold war era." The Carter administration was in effect endeavoring to "rent" the services and resources of the Pakistani state once again (Haqqani 2006)!

In India, the return of Mrs Gandhi soon aroused the old irritations in Washington when she proved unwilling to issue a blanket denunciation of the invasion. The most the Indian side would say was that they "regretted" what had taken place and hoped for a "peaceful resolution." External Affairs Minister Narasimha Rao confided to me that when Gromyko visited New Delhi from February 12 to 14, he told him, "You are making it difficult for your friends to help you." As regards the Clifford trip to New Delhi, the U.S. interpretation was that the emissary's presence "was appreciated." However not long after this, in a conversation in South Block, the External Affairs minister asked me who Clark Clifford was, and appeared to be unclear about his actual political importance. Then he told me that this "old man" said that if you are concerned about the United States giving USD 400 million in military aid to Pakistan, the United States would be willing to give India an equal amount. Rao said he was taken aback by this statement and replied, as noted earlier, that he felt the best solution would be for the United States to abstain from introducing any more military wherewithal into the region. This is a version that has been vociferously denied by U.S. officials; one, however, because of my long friendship with the late External Affairs Minister, I tend to believe.

Soon, however, the Reagan Administration would enter the wings and for a time bring with it a quite different atmosphere to U.S.–Indian relations.

9

THE REAGAN ADMINISTRATION (1981–1989)

While Ronald Reagan's ascendancy to the American presidency in 1980 intensified American involvement in Afghanistan and the aggressive utilization of Pakistan as a base for promoting the Afghan insurgency against the Soviet occupation, it did not impel a complete return to the levels of piquish politics, which had characterized past U.S.–Indian relations. This is because perspective changes had occurred on both sides. The Reagan administration, in a new spirit of measured bilateralism that actually commenced during the Ford administration, succeeded, as Stephen P. Cohen notes, in forging a "limited strategic relationship" with Pakistan which did not at the same time, despite Narasimha Rao's prior reservations, "commit the United States against India but did stiffen Pakistani resistance against the Soviets." While the Carter administration had adopted a highly moralistic stance on nonproliferation issues, which held to ransom almost every other policy concern in the U.S. portfolio *vis-à-vis* South Asia, the Reagan administration decided that a dose of real politik had more to offer. The idea was that if India and Pakistan were dealt within a more business-like, essentially nonideological, fashion, receiving from the United States the kind of assistance and cooperation that each deemed important to their security requirements, consistent, of course, with American security interests, then neither state would feel an urgent need to build the bomb (Cohen 1992: 149).

Probably Indira Gandhi's assassination in 1984, which ultimately led to the political ascent of her son, Rajiv Gandhi, was destined to play a greater role than many realize in reinforcing this trend toward less invasive and strident diplomacy. The Rajiv Gandhi regime ignited optimism not only about the prospects for an improved security environment, but for crucial economic changes as well, which if implemented augured well for greater long-term compatibility in the Indo-American relationship.

Rajiv's visit to the United States in 1985 greatly intensified these expectations because at this point he had

Photograph 9.1: Indian Prime Minister Indira Gandhi with U.S. President Ronald Reagan during her 1982 visit to U.S.

established a reputation as a modern, "can-do," new-generation Indian politician who, as P.V. Narasimha Rao put it (personal conversation) functioned in a kind of "chairman of the board" style. Especially among the younger generation of Indians there was a feeling that Rajiv would inaugurate a new era of prosperity; he captured their imagination for a time. Reagan was "impressed" with Rajiv. "Personal chemistry between Reagan and Rajiv Gandhi was exceptional," declares Tahir-Kheli. He interpreted Rajiv's emphasis on high-tech as a "pragmatic desire to go to the best source" and "as reflecting a change in the international environment" (Tahir-Kehli 1997: 73).

Photograph 9.2: Prime Minister Rajiv Gandhi receives from U.S. Ambassador John Gunther Dean the first copy of a book commemorating 40 years of Indo-U.S. Cooperation

Even before Rajiv's visit, there had been signs of a new mood in Indo-U.S. relations, which had reverberated all the way to Capitol Hill. Conservative Senator Orin Hatch sang India's praises on the floor of the United States Senate. "I believe a historic shift is underway," he had intoned. He went on to say, "Ten years from now scholars will look back on this last year as the end to the Ice Age ... "

However, Rajiv Gandhi, due to his political inexperience, had pretty much lost control both of his agenda

Photograph 9.3: U.S. President Ronald Reagan and his wife welcome Indian Prime Minister Rajiv Gandhi and his wife at the White House on June 12, 1985

and the Congress Party by the end of his tenure in 1989 when Congress was voted out of office by the Janata Dal coalition led by V.P. Singh. This proved to be a very unstable phase in Indian politics, which saw the rapid rise and fall of three prime ministers (*viz.*, Rajiv Gandhi, V.P. Singh, and Chandra Shekhar) within a four-year time span (1989–1993). The denouement of these tumultuous times was Rajiv's assassination (May 21, 1991) while campaigning for a return to office. His successor, P.V. Narasimha Rao (1991–1996), proved to be politically durable and got the Congress Party and the

Photograph 9.4: Prime Minister Rajiv Gandhi with President Ronald Reagan outside the White House on October 20, 1987

country back on track, no doubt because the forces driving change both within India and around the world were proving to be irresistible. The world was on the cusp of the dawning global economy, very much influenced by the impact of so-called "Reaganomics"; Rao clearly foresaw its economic and strategic implications and commenced the process of moving his country toward a more deregulated economy and a more flexible, pragmatic diplomacy.

In our private conversations it was clear that he was prepared to edge India away from two generations of bureaucratized, overcentralized "post-office socialism" (Ambassador Galbraith's term) at a time when few in the Congress Party could accept such a proposition. But Rao was realistic about it. Thus, even though the reforms he actually initiated were far less comprehensive than many critics thought were needed, the economic liberalization policies begun during his prime ministership (eventually leading to the rise of Manmohan Singh) must be seen retrospectively as a watershed marking the point where significant structural changes in the Indian economy commenced and consequently fundamental structural differentiation between India and Pakistan became immanent. In my last conversation with Narasimha Rao, shortly before his death, I suggested that his role in opening the door to economic liberalization and greater political flexibility in the international arena, was structurally comparable to the role that Gorbachev played in the Soviet Union and Dung Shao Ping played in China. He did not disagree.

Coupled with the continued success of democratic government in India, and its failure in Pakistan, the changes underway once and for all undermined the American rationale for mindlessly treating India and Pakistan simply as two equally culpable rivals enmeshed in a symbiotic political *danse macabre*. The two states were now gravitating in very different directions— India toward increasing economic prosperity, political stability, and international respectability; Pakistan toward economic stagnation, political instability, enmeshment in the world of international terrorism, and the institutionalization of its status as a "strategic landlord."

The mounting intensity of the Afghan war must be seen as the principal catalyst for this growing post-Cold War differentiation. The eventual defeat of the Soviet invasion was a "stinger-missile victory" achieved by Muslim radicals ideologically driven by Wahabism, bankrolled by the United States and the oil-rich Gulf states (particularly Saudi Arabia), whose base of operations was Pakistan. In the end, this force would replace Bolshevism as the pervasive doctrinal challenge to Western secularism, and transform Pakistan into a nuclear-armed, conspiratorial state tacitly, if not overtly, where it would be held hostage to, if indeed not act in overt collusion with, the new Islamic radicalism.

But the culmination of this newly configuring challenge to U.S. hegemony still lay in the future, considerably beyond the issues and challenges immediately confronting what remained of Ronald Reagan's political tenure. By Reagan's second term, the debate over South Asia policy was gravitating toward a complex interplay between Congress and the White House, concerning the former's preoccupation with nuclear nonproliferation and the latter's preoccupation with keeping Pakistan in the Cold War camp despite its obvious determination to acquire nuclear weapons. Underlyingly it reflected doctrinal and policy differences between a Democratic Congress and a Republican administration. This cleavage would come to the forefront in the succeeding Bush-1 and Clinton administrations.

10

THE BUSH-1 ADMINISTRATION (1989–1993)

George Herbert Walker Bush, fellow Republican Ronald Reagan's vice-president, succeeded him as president in 1989. As it turned out, the Bush-1 administration became preoccupied with the Gulf War that was waged against Iraq to undo Saddam Hussein's invasion and occupation of Kuwait. Relatively speaking, therefore, South Asia policy remained on the back burner.

Thus, the early years of the 1990s can be characterized as a comparatively quiescent period from this standpoint. Yet beneath the surface things were far from tranquil; a storm was gathering that was destined eventually to profoundly affect America's relations with the region. A great deal of social, political, and economic ferment was occurring in India and Pakistan, which soon would have widespread ramifications both for the Subcontinent and the United States. In India, the political spectrum was beginning to gravitate toward the Right, away from the Fabian Socialism of the Nehru era and toward deregulation and market economics, and toward a more strident Hindu chauvinism, which at times called into question some aspects of Indian secularism itself. The old automatic Congress Party parliamentary majorities were giving way to multiparty coalitions, which denied ideological monopolies to any single political group. Even in cases where Congress remained the largest component of such coalitions this was the case. Provincial and regionally based parties reflecting a wide variety of doctrinal and material predilections, whether or not Congress was dominant in them, were increasingly compelled to govern through intense bargaining processes and uneasy consensus that satisfied everyone somewhat and nobody completely. It was in this atmosphere of crystallizing change and emerging new challenges that the George H.W. Bush's presidency (1989–1993) in the United States and the prime ministership of P.V. Narasimha Rao in India (1991 to 1996) took shape. Rao's was the last Congress government that endured for a full five-year term, and the first whose majorities were so tenuous that the only way it could survive for a full term was by negotiating crass deals almost on a daily basis with marginally loyal factions whose defection could bring the party down at the drop of a hat. This resulted in a series of scandals throughout Rao's tenure, such as the bribing of five Jharkhandi MPs in 1993 in order to keep them in camp and maintain Congress's slim parliamentary majority.

Also, as Bush-1 was assuming office, the trend in Pakistan was toward political disarray and a renewal of military dictatorship. Although it was not fully realized at the time, India was becoming the world's first concerted target of Islamic jihadism. Terrorists, whose ideology and methodologies had been formed in the crucible of the Afghan War, were being provided asylum, training and staging by Pakistan's Inter-Services Intelligence Agency (ISI) and then funneled into Kashmir to wage war against India's alleged "occupation" of that disputed state. Hundreds were being killed in Kashmir, as the precursors of Al Qaeda systematically fomented insurrection there and helped drive the heretofore dominant Pandits out of the Valley. These Pakistani sponsored terrorist bands were morphing into Al Qaeda formations as Rao and Bush-1 were assuming office. These terrorists would detonate a series of seven bomb blasts in Mumbai's financial district on March 1, 1993, a month after another off-shoot of Al Qaeda exploded a car bomb in the World Trade Center in New York; both were milestones ineluctably leading to 9/11 a decade later, and the Mumbai massacre on November 26, 2008.

In Washington, South Asia policy became centered on a contest between White House "real politik," on the one hand, and a combination of "moral politics" and "special interests politics" emanating from the U.S. Congress, on the other. The purpose was to determine where a *modus vivendi* could be struck between the political flexibility, which the White House understandably believed was necessary to effectively conduct practical day-to-day foreign policy, while, nevertheless, in deference to humanitarian considerations, maintaining a semblance of the nonproliferation regimens, which key members of the U.S. Congress deemed essential to prevent a nuclear holocaust. By the time of the Bush-1 administration this contest between competing forces had crystallized into loosely organized "lobbies."

One was the so-called "India Caucus" on Capitol Hill. It had undergone a revival and enlargement in scope in direct proportion to what was perceived to be the renewed influence of the "Pakistan lobby" that was garnering support from an administration increasingly inclined to bend the nonproliferation rules in exchange for Pakistani cooperation amidst the rising specter of Islamic fundamentalism and terrorism in Afghanistan, in Africa and across the Middle East. From the administration's standpoint it was a matter of seeking ways to circumvent orthodox nonproliferation strictures, authored by Senators Symington, Glenn, and Pressler, sufficiently to keep a politically shaky Pakistan in the strategic game despite its obviously secretive back-sliding on nuclear weaponization, while at the same time attempting to deter an increasingly politically and economically assertive India from escalating its nuclear program in response to developments in Pakistan.

The Pressler Amendment (enacted in 1984) to the Nuclear Non-Proliferation Act of 1978 ordained that no further aid or military sales could be provided either to Pakistan or India if they acquired, or seemed determined to acquire, nuclear weapons. When Afghanistan occurred, the United States was legally barred from sending arms to Pakistan. The way around this impediment was what may be called the reification of ambiguity or "waivers diplomacy." With the India lobby in opposition, the U.S. Senate, at the administration's behest, achieved a compromise, "at eleven o'clock at night on December 31, 1987," by adopting an initiative by Senators Inouye, Kasten, Moynihan, and Pell "which dropped all references to India and effectively gave Pakistan a six-year waiver of the Symington and Glenn amendments on the condition that the president certify annually that termination of assistance to that country would damage the national security of the United States" (Gould 2001: 144–215; Rubinoff 2001: 199–200). The Bush-1 administration stuck to this latter day Reagan administration initiative throughout its four-year tenure while obviously doing its utmost to conceal or play down suspected Pakistani circumventions of the rules.

India did not take the Bush-1 administration's "waivers diplomacy" and its resultant replenishment of Pakistan's military capabilities lying down. As in the past, it pursued measures for balancing the strategic equation. Along with shoring up its conventional military ties with the Soviet Union (*i.e.*, advanced weapons purchases), it is now conceded that this also paved the way for the Pokhran nuclear tests that ultimately occurred on Atal Behari Vajpayee's watch in 1998. These policies reached fruition well after Bush-1's term in office ended in 1993, but his pursuit of "waivers diplomacy" to sustain Pakistan's role in the Afghan War and its immediate aftermath was perhaps the most important role at that time that his administration played in U.S.–Indian relations.

There was, however, one other undertaking initiated by Bush-1, which essentially was a spin-off from the waivers diplomacy phase. This was the decision to initiate a dialogue with India whose purpose was to deepen the strategic relationship between India and the United States; through this it was hoped that whatever concessions the Bush administration believed it must make to keep Pakistan in the game would be counterbalanced and compensated by a series of interlocked initiatives that would reassure India about the depth and sincerity of America's commitment to mutual security and long-term support of India's desire to end for once and for all the atmosphere of pique, which had for so long dogged relations between the world's two greatest democracies. These were termed the *Next Steps in Strategic Partnership (NSSP)*. The rationale for this initiative was expressed by Christina R. Rocca, Assistant Secretary of State for South Asian Affairs, before the House Committee on International Relations on June 22, 2004. "As India increases its global reach, we are working to build an effective strategic partnership . . . Our long term strategic interests dictate that we pursue this goal."

However, it would be William Jefferson Clinton, George Herbert Walker Bush's successor, who was destined to be the first American president to directly confront the new forces, which the emerging global economy and the rise of Islamic radicalism had set in motion.

11

THE CLINTON ADMINISTRATION (1993–2001)

I n historical retrospect, we can say that the Clinton administration, perhaps as much by happenstance as by design, at long last commenced the final transition in South Asian diplomacy from the militarized grand strategy promulgated by John Foster Dulles and the Cold War hawks in the 1950s to the more nuanced diplomacy that now regards India as a key strategic partner, while Pakistan continues to be treated as the fragile reed that it has always been; as a state on the brink of political disaster, beset with internal contradictions that seem at any moment to plunge her into self-destruction.

During Clinton's first term (1993–1997) it was more or less "business as usual" as far as South Asia policy was concerned. Coping with the policy dilemmas inherited from his predecessors, including the debate between Congress and the White House over what should be the appropriate admixture of pragmatism (*i.e.*, "wavers diplomacy") and nonproliferation orthodoxy (*i.e.*, "moral diplomacy"), were the administration's most compelling concerns. As his second term (1997–2001) unfolded, however, a host of new issues surfaced, both within and outside South Asia. Outside the region was genocide in the Balkans, plus developments in East Africa, which by 1998 culminated in Mogadishu (Somalia), the embassy bombings in Dar es Salaam and Nairobi, the attack on the USS Cole in Aden (2000), and the retaliatory missile strikes against Al Qaeda training camps in Afghanistan. At home, in addition to foreign policy, there was also Mr Clinton's "personal problems," which led to his attempted impeachment by the U.S. Congress.

Despite these multifarious distractions, however, Clinton was compelled to remain attentive to the challenges confronting him in South Asia, especially in the light of the presence of terrorism along the region's perimeter and in the Pakistan heartland. It was also clear to his policy team and other close observers of the South Asia scene that a new round of proliferation was in the air. Pakistani operatives had been exposed shopping for nuclear technology and relevant hardware from Texas to Pyongyang. American intelligence was sure that the Indians were preparing for nuclear weapons tests at Pokhran in the near future. With everyone expecting both South Asian states to explicitly become nuclear states at any moment, the principal U.S. foreign policy preoccupation became how to prevent it if possible or contain it once it happened.

The administration groped for answers to these numerous challenges that it faced both within the region and at home, especially in the halls of the U.S. Congress. A number of factors were in play in South Asia—*viz.*, mounting terrorism and political turmoil in Pakistan (the fall of Benazir Bhutto, the rise and fall of Nawaz

Photograph 11.1: Prime Minister P.V. Narasimha Rao and President Bill Clinton on May 19, 1994

Sharif, factional restiveness in the Paki military); and, in India, a rising tide of Hindu nationalism driven by the BJP, energized by communal events like the *Babri Masjid* incident, and the evocative impact of a TV miniseries apotheosizing the *Mahabharata* (see Hardgraves 1993: 291-293; Rudolph 1993: 436-454). Less than two years into Clinton's second term (1998), an electoral stalemate had resulted when the Rao government lost its majority and had to be replaced by a new coalition with I.K. Gujral as interim prime minister pending new elections. Following those elections, *Hindutva* (a coalition dominated by the BJP) had become the dominant policy of government, with Atal Behari Vajpayee as Prime Minister, and remained so throughout the remainder of his administration.

The coming of the Vajpayee government in many respects turned out to be a salutary development from the standpoint of U.S.-Indian relations. Under the impact of globalization and in response to ongoing deregulation and marketization of the Indian economy, plus the growth and socioeconomic importance of South Asian Indians in the United States, a new centrist atmosphere emerged, which yielded a significant degree of amity, an absence of pique, and a further measure of the strategic compatibility, which NSSP had initiated. These trends were also abetted by the rising tide of Islamic extremism and terrorism affecting both countries—in India Kashmir, in the United States just about everywhere.

Photograph 11.2: Secretary of State Ms Albright and Prime Minister I.K. Gujral holding broadbased discussions

It was at this point that the famous "dialogue" commenced between Prime Minister Vajpayee's finance minister, Jaswant Singh, and President Clinton's representative, deputy assistant secretary of state, Strobe Talbott, that continued for more than two years and embraced fourteen formal and numerous informal encounters for the purpose of trying to resolve the pattern of "estrangement" that had so long dogged U.S.–Indian relations (Talbott 2004). This especially pertained to nonproliferation matters, where it was apparent to everyone that both India and Pakistan were on the verge of deploying nuclear weapons. This process actually commenced in May of 1998 at Chagai and Pokhran, respectively.

Valiant attempts had been made by Clinton through Talbott and other administration officials to induce both states to forego taking this final step, and instead sign the *CTBT*,[1] by offering them relief from sanctions imposed by the Glenn and Pressler amendments and other inducements. In the case of Pakistan this even extended to reinstating the sale of the interdicted F16 fighter bombers along with other conventional weaponry; an offer, of course, that outraged India. Prime Minister P.V. Narasimha Rao, however, agreed to abort weapons tests that were already in the works when he made his official visit to the United States on May 19, 1994. Clinton and Talbott used his presence in Washington to persuade him to do this in order to avoid sanctions and other obstacles that would inhibit his plans and those of Manmohan Singh, his then finance minister (now India's prime minister), to liberalize and marketize the Indian economy. This was a matter that I knew to be dear to his heart because Rao and I, as fellow democratic socialists who believed that orthodox Socialism sorely needed ideological detoxification, had personally discussed many times over the years.

When the Democrats lost control of both houses of Congress in 1994, Clinton's latitude for maneuver on inducing India and Pakistan to forego nuclear weaponization by signing the *CTBT* was severely undermined when the Republican majority refused to ratify the treaty. This obviously emboldened the Hindu nationalist regime in India, and the India-phobic Pakistani regime, to be far more resistant to doing so. That resistance, however delicately asserted by the consummately civilized Jaswant Singh, became the touchstone of the prolonged dialogue between them. In the end, however, I suggest that the mooting of the *CTBT* actually contributed to more pragmatic, less ideologically strident negotiations. Talbott himself disagrees with this assessment for what I believe are understandable reasons from his standpoint—*viz.*, his commitment to a formal agreement. However, Talbott's own account of the dialogue shows that had it been ratified the Clinton administration would have had made any concessions they made to India on sanctions conditional on the Indians signing the *CTBT*, something they were implacably opposed to doing. Since the United States itself now had feet of clay in the matter, it was no longer in a position to be so self-righteous about it, which, in my opinion, facilitated the many interim understandings that actually were achieved.

Pakistan, predictably by default, provided the impetus for dramatic changes that got the stalemated nonproliferation dialogue off dead center. It was Kargil, Pakistan sponsored terrorism in Kashmir (termed "guest terrorists," by former ambassador to Washington, Naresh Chandra), the fall and exile of Prime Minister Nawaz Sharif, the Musharraf coup, and the resurgence of military dictatorship, that finally opened Mr Clinton's eyes and caused him to tailor U.S. policy to the ugly reality of a failing Pakistani state and a contrasting politically viable Indian state. He continued to search for a *modus operandi* with Pakistan in the name of her curious status as a *Major Non-NATO Ally*, but primary stress henceforth was laid on the burgeoning relationship between India and the United States.

This perceptual shift consummated in President Clinton's South Asia trip on March 19, 2000. His impact was stunning in India and dismaying in Pakistan. His condemnation of a recent terrorist massacre in a Sikh village won him much favor. But his speech before the Indian parliament was a rhetorical triumph. "Clinton read the mood of the approximately seven hundred men and women in front of him and recrafted parts of the speech as he talked"(Talbott 2004: 199).

En route home, the President literally sneaked into Pakistan, symbolizing thereby the moral distinction he made between the two states. He briefly met with Musharraf, and gave a fifteen minute speech, "televised live and in full so that Musharraf would not be able to pick and choose which passages were aired" (ibid.: 205).

A new course in South Asian policy had been set which the Bush-2 administration would carry forward.

12

THE BUSH-2 ADMINISTRATION (2001–2009)

W hen George Walker Bush won office as the 43rd president of the United States, after a bruising election whose outcome is disputed to this day, no one could have imagined that his administration was destined to have a greater impact on U.S.–Indian relations than any since President Eisenhower's first term. And happily for the opposite reasons: The things that Dwight Eisenhower's Secretary of State, John Foster Dulles, did to poison the relationship between the world's two largest democracies in 1953, were at last rectified by the political sagacity of George Bush's secretary of state, Condoleeza Rice, two generations later, when President Bush and Prime Minister Manmohan Singh signed the agreement on nuclear cooperation on July 18, 2005, during the Prime Minister's visit to Washington. Later, on March 2, 2006, during President Bush's trip to New Delhi, the finalization of India's nuclear separation plan occurred.

Thus, the Bush administration brought to fruition the initiatives that his immediate predecessor, Bill Clinton, had sown, and with this finally put to rest the last vestiges of the Cold War in South Asia.

There were indications as early as President Bush's first election campaign that those advising him on South Asia policy were inclining him toward propounding a new approach to India that would build on the changed atmosphere, which President Clinton's resounding visit to New Delhi in 2000 had created. Informed opinion in Washington was predicting that Bush was prepared to heed urgings by the "India Caucus," co-chaired by Republican Senator Sam Brownback and Democratic Congressman Jim McDermott, to lift post-Pokhran sanctions as soon as possible and commence working toward a "new strategic relationship" between the two countries. Along with the 120-member caucus was the emergent lobbying power of the two million strong Indian-American community, which some said had become as effective on the Hill as the so-called Jewish lobby. One news account stated on January 10, 2001, shortly after Bush took office, that McDermott was "confident" that the president would lift the sanctions. "The general feeling in Congress," McDermott declared, "is that sanctions are not a very effective tool in a world moving toward globalization." The story went on to say that "relations were expected to be built up from the Clinton visit to India, and Prime Minister Atal Bihari Vajpayee's visit to the U.S. last year."

Bush, in any event, had bluntly stated during the campaign that if elected he would favor an immediate lifting of all sanctions, and would not pressure India to sign the *CTBT*. Condoleeza Rice, slated to chair the *National Security Council (NSC)*, and eventually to become Secretary of State, declared that U.S. foreign policy toward India had thus far been "wasted years" due to Washington's "obsession" with nuclear proliferation, Pakistan, and Kashmir rather than focus on "broader issues" like India's potential place as a stabilizing force in South Asia. Richard Haas, who served with Rice on the *NSC*, characterized the Republican platform with respect to South Asia as more "future oriented" than the Democratic.

The Bush administration stuck to its guns after the election was over. What is especially striking about this is the fact that South Asia policy had so many competitors for Mr Bush's attention. Foremost, of course, was 9/11, and its companion piece, the Iraq war. There were undoubtedly two reasons why South Asia remained on the table, apart from the lobbying input of Indian-Americans. One was the specter of jihadist terrorism, which haunted both India and America, and in which Pakistan was implicated via both Afghanistan and Kashmir. The other was India's spectacular entry into the global economy and the importance this assumed for the powerful American corporate community. Reasons had arisen why neither the United States nor India could any longer afford the politics of pique; they had come to need each other in new ways that could only be

Photograph 12.1: U.S. President George W. Bush, left, meets with Pakistan's President Pervez Musharraf on the sidelines of the United Nations General Assembly in New York, Wednesday, September 22, 2004

Photograph 12.2: Pakistani opposition leader Benazir Bhutto, right, poses for a photo with U.S. Ambassador Anne W. Patterson, left, after their meeting at Bhutto's residence in Karachi on Monday, November 19, 2007

actualized through political reconciliation and strategic compatibility.

In this sense, Jaswant Singh's holding action against signing the *CTBT* during the "dialogue" with Strobe Talbott preserved maneuvering room within which the Bush administration's "future oriented" diplomacy could be deployed. Otherwise India would have been locked into a more narrowly constructed, sanctions-ridden regimen that would have been more difficult to maneuver through. Unencumbered by these structural impediments, incoming Secretary of State Colin Powell lifted an array of sanctions on September 22, 2001, under the rubric of a "Memorandum of Justification," which conformed to Congressional requirements for such action.

A terrorist attack on the Indian parliament emanating from Pakistan on December 13, 2001, and an outbreak of communal strife in Godhra (Gujarat) on February 27, 2002, for a time threatened to disrupt progress toward stability, but their repercussions were contained and negotiations on the larger strategic picture continued

Photograph 12.3: President Bush meets with Pakistani President Asif Ali Zardari in New York, Tuesday, September 23, 2008. The president is scheduled to address the United Nations General Assembly later today

on track. Colin Powell's trip to Pakistan in March 2004, in which Pakistan was designated a *Major Non-NATO Ally*, did nothing to help U.S.–Indian reconciliation; but this too was overcome once it was clear that in substantive terms it did not connote any resumption of old fashioned Cold War diplomacy in the Subcontinent.

There were rumblings of discontent in both the American and Indian camps as negotiations on the strategic agreement proceeded. Many scientists and hard-line nationalists expressed opposition to any arrangement that would inhibit India's sovereignty and ability to engage in whatever measure of nuclear development they deemed essential to Indian security. The former Chairman of the Atomic Energy Regulatory Board, Gopalakrishnan, declared that Americans cannot be trusted and labeled his colleagues who went along with them as "stupid analysts."

Critics on the American side essentially believed that India was gaining too much at a bargain price in terms of conformity to international nonproliferation protocols. Michael Krepon of the Stimson Center called it a "Sweetheart deal for India." *Guardian* columnist Jonathan Steele accused the Bush administration of "rewarding India with a nuclear deal."

Happily for India and the Indian American community, which had worked so hard for it, President Bush and Prime Minister Manmohan Singh affirmed the "historic agreement," as noted, during Manmohan's visit to Washington. It now requires ratification by the U.S. Congress, which most believe will eventually take place despite the changes wrought by the ensuing mid-term elections and Mr Obama's ascent to the presidency. At a joint press conference, President Bush declared, "What this agreement says is that things change, times change, that leadership can make a difference." Prime Minister Singh said simply, "We have made history today and I thank you." Clearly he was correct since half a century of pique and misunderstanding between India and the United States appeared to be drawing to an end.

POSTSCRIPT

THE 13th AMERICAN PRESIDENT

As this slim volume goes to press, a new general election has occurred in the United States. The new American President, Barack Obama, was inaugurated on January 13, 2009. He was immediately compelled to craft relationships with India and Pakistan which reflected the escalating impact of Islamic jihadism throughout the region, especially in Afghanistan and Hindu Kush. The choice had been between either Barack Obama, the first African-American to run for the presidency on one of the two major political parties, or Republican John McCain, a war hero of Vietnam vintage who was imprisoned for five years, and suffered mightily, at the hands of the Viet Minh in the infamous "Hanoi Hilton."

There were strong differences between these two men, especially on issues of war and peace, on U.S.–India relations, and international diplomacy in general.

The winner's policies will impact differentially on U.S.–Indian relations, and not insignificantly.

Mr Obama based the foreign policy aspect of his presidential campaign on a pledge to expeditiously terminate the U.S. military presence in Iraq and place greater emphasis on defeating the Taliban and Al Qaeda in Pakistan and Afghanistan. In this connection, Obama has already gone on record with a promise that he will more aggressively pursue the jihadis who have now established themselves as a terrorist quasi-state in the border regions between Pakistan and Afghanistan. His decision to enlarge the U.S. military presence in the region by 30,000 troops stresses his determination to deliver the political goods.

With respect to American policy toward Iraq and Afghanistan, under an Obama administration, the candidate pledged that he would visit the region prior to the election and base his final conclusions about what must be done upon the situation he found existing on the ground there. He made hasty visits to the Middle East more to establish his *bona fides* as a foreign policy-cognizant politician than to accomplish anything concrete policy-wise. During the campaign, Obama spoke by phone with Iraq's Foreign Minister, Hoshyar Zebari, and declared, "I emphasized to him how encouraged I was by the reductions in violence in Iraq, but also insisted that it is important for us to begin the process of withdrawing U.S. troops, making clear that we have no interest in permanent bases in Iraq" (*CNN*, June 17, 2008). This was a clear indication that under his presidency the messianic mission of the Bush administration to impose the so-called "American Dream" on the Middle East, will be brought to an end and replaced by more measured, mature approaches emphasizing cooperation and consensus among the many countries, including India, who are concerned with achieving political stability in the Middle East and South Asia; wherever possible this would include participation by the United Nations and other multinational bodies like *NATO*.

Such an approach would offer considerable scope for the world's two largest democracies to pursue collaborative and mutually beneficial initiatives across a wide spectrum of international challenges, ranging from nuclear proliferation (especially pertaining to Iran) to terrorism, and the creation of oil and natural gas pipelines, which promise to forge a vast and challenging network of economic and political links between South, Southeast, and Inner Asia on a scale unimaginable even two decades ago.

There have been no indications that Mr Obama would not endeavor to pursue the U.S.–Indian strategic relationship as this has evolved under the Bush administration.

Concerning Pakistan specifically, Mr Obama has publicly chided the country's leadership for failing to deal decisively with the pursuit of Osama Bin Laden.

Photograph PS-1: President Barack Obama meets with India's Prime Minister Manmohan Singh at the G-20 summit at the ExCel Centre in London. India has watched with wariness as President Barack Obama's administration has lavished attention on rivals Pakistan and China. Now, Obama is trying to ease Indian worries by honoring Prime Minister Manmohan Singh on Tuesday, November 24, 2009 with the first state visit of his presidency

He went on record to declare that he would not hesitate to authorize a military strike into Waziristan if an accurate sighting of the Al Qaeda leader should occur. As I stated in an India Abroad article on September 27, 2007, "Understandably, this has caused a stir in Islamabad and has prompted Obama's rivals in both political parties to accuse him of all the usual things that are standard fare for political rivals in search of an electoral advantage."

Quite to the contrary, however, Mr Obama's orientation to the Pakistan conundrum has an air of authenticity about it. His presidency would seem to herald a decisive end to any further American blank check tolerance of military dictatorship in that country. Mr Obama seems to be saying that the long-standing *modus vivendi*, which for half a century has allowed the Pakistani ruling elite to have its political cake and eat it must end once and for all; that a new policy disposition will make American support for Pakistan dependent upon whether it creates latitude for genuine civilian government and serious efforts to eliminate the Taliban-Al Qaeda asylum in the Hindu Kush. The priority should be, he declared (*India Abroad*, February 29, 2008), "to do more to roll back the Al Qaeda sanctuary," without putting all our eggs in the Musharraf basket. "Assistance to Pakistan should be conditional, in order to encourage strong action against Al Qaeda and a restoration of democracy in that country."

Another advantage, which President Obama brings to the table is his multicultural and multiracial credentials. The offspring of a Kenyan father and a middle-class White woman from the middle-western state of Kansas, Obama spent some of his early childhood years living in the Third World—in Indonesia where he attended elementary school in predominantly Muslim educational institutions while his mother did anthropological fieldwork there in pursuit of her doctoral degree in this field. He then spent his later childhood and adolescence in Hawaii, another multicultural, multiracial environment. He also spent time in Kenya trying to establish meaningful ties with his late father's kinsmen, something he discusses at length and with great poignancy in his remarkable auto-biographical book, *Dreams from my Father*.

These socialization experiences make Mr Obama the most culturally unique among all American presidents who have preceded him, and the most instinctively inter-nationally oriented president in American history. His sensitivity to the political and cultural nuances of the Third World bode nothing but good for the future of U.S. relations both with India and Pakistan.

Senator John McCain, the Republican nominee for U.S. Presidentship, hails from a very different social, cul-tural, and political background. He is the scion of three generations of high ranking naval officers. It is well known that as a fighter-bomber pilot during the Vietnam War he was shot down and imprisoned for five years in the infamous "Hanoi Hilton" prison, where he was subjected to unspeakable torture and duress. Once re-turned to the United States, Mr McCain won election to the U.S. House of Representatives and then the U.S. Senate. His political career won him in some measure the image of a "maverick," who has not always hued to the neoconservative political doctrines and policies, which the Bush administration pursued, and led to the controversial invasion of Iraq. However, Mr McCain's differences with the Bush administration were never over the invasion of Iraq *per se* but over their unsuccessful ability to consolidate their conquest and achieve their stated goal of bringing American style democracy to the region. He advocated throughout his campaign an indefinite military involvement in Iraq and at the same time pledged if elected President to pursue conservative economic policies at home that essentially would further abet the process of transferring wealth to the corporate elite in the name of a radical form of *carte blanch* "trickle-down economics," which would allegedly, but controversially, impart prosperity to American society writ large. The current collapse of America's financial markets and skyrocketing unemployment stand in mute testimony to the ruinous implications of such policies.

There is one aspect of the incumbent Obama administration, which invokes some unease in India about the future of U.S.–Indian relations. It pertains to the identity of many of the advisors who appear to be on deck to join the Obama administration in foreign policy capacities. As far as South Asia is concerned, Siddharth Varadarajan (*The Hindu*, November 6, 2008) points out that several of these individuals evoke "unhappy memories" of the roles they played during past administrations on issues like nonproliferation, "hypenization," and Kashmir. These include Anthony Lake, Strobe Talbott, Robert Einhorn, Richard Holbrooke, Karl Inderfurth, and even Vice-President Joe Biden. On these issues, "India has reason to be cautious." How energetically might some of these advisors make India's continued strategic partnership with the United States dependent upon her signing the *CTBT* before she deems it to be in her strategic interest to do so? Could events in Kashmir take an ugly turn that would induce the Obama administration to appoint an "American special envoy . . . something that would slice through the 'strategic partnership' like a hot knife through butter?" Could the war against the Taliban/Al Qaeda escalate to such proportions that the U.S. military relationship with Pakistan would result in a "re-hypenization" of India and Pakistan in U.S. South Asia policy?

These are clearly possible eventualities that could draw the Obama administration in part or in whole back into the pre-Clinton and pre-Bush policy mode. However, the chances of this occurring do not seem to be great given the apparent level of Mr Obama's intellectual depth, and the economic, political, and strategic resources that have been built up over the past decade-and-a-half. In Varadarajan's words, it is unlikely that "an Obama administration will risk jeopardizing the gains Washington has already made through the Bush years by pursuing policies on terrorism, Kashmir and the economy which would alienate India."

Notes

Chapter 1

1. Pakistan, by contrast, hesitated to go as far as India along this path, in part because of the attraction of its leaders to Islamic theocratic predilections and in part because the dominant elites who inherited power in the new state were predominantly landed aristocracies, traditional bureaucrats, and members of an officer corps steeped in the norms of the old colonial culture all of whom who saw mass politics as a threat to their sense of public order and privilege. The result was a failure to carry constitutional development beyond the limited franchise, "viceregal" constitutional structure, which the British and the nationalists had negotiated in 1935 but which India undertook to supercede as soon as freedom had been won. In India, this democratization process consummated in the 1950 Constitution of India, one of the most comprehensive democratic constitutions ever written. In Pakistan, by contrast, the retention of a limited franchise constitution, which preserved the dominance and privileges of the elite classes resulted in an autocratic/paternalistic pattern of government which by 1959 culminated in the country's first (but not last) military dictatorship (under General Ayub Khan). This difference between the type of government chosen by each state was destined to be a crucial factor in determining America's differential orientation to India and Pakistan over the ensuing years.

2. The Marshall Plan (from its enactment, officially the European Recovery Program [ERP]) was the primary plan of the United States for rebuilding and creating a stronger foundation for

the allied countries of Europe, and repelling communism after World War II. The initiative was named for U.S. Secretary of State George Marshall and was largely the creation of State Department officials, especially William L. Clayton and George F. Kennan.

The reconstruction plan was developed at a meeting of the participating European states on July 12, 1947. The Marshall Plan offered the same aid to the Soviet Union and its allies, if they would make political reforms and accept certain outside controls. However the Soviet Union rejected this proposal with Vyacheslav Molotov describing the plan as dollar imperialism.

The plan was in operation for four years beginning in July 1947. During that period some USD13 billion of economic and technical assistance was given to help the recovery of the European countries that had joined in the Organization for Economic Co-operation and Development.

3. The *North Atlantic Treaty Organisation* (*NATO*; French: *Organisation du Traité de* l'Atlantique Nord ["OTAN"]; also called the North Atlantic Alliance, the Atlantic Alliance, or the Western Alliance) is a military alliance established by the signing of the North Atlantic Treaty on April 4, 1949. With headquarters in Brussels, Belgium, the organization established a system of collective security whereby its member states agreed to mutual defense in response to an attack by any external party.

The Treaty of Brussels, signed on March 17, 1948 by Belgium, the Netherlands, Luxembourg, France, and the United Kingdom, is considered the precursor to the *NATO* agreement. This treaty established a military alliance, later to become the Western European Union. However, American participation was thought necessary in order to counter the military power of the Soviet Union, and therefore talks for a new military alliance began almost immediately.

These talks resulted in the North Atlantic Treaty, created by Lester B. Pearson, which was signed in Washington, DC on

April 4, 1949. It included the five Treaty of Brussels states, as well as the United States, Canada, Portugal, Italy, Norway, Denmark, and Iceland. Three years later, on February 18, 1952, Greece and Turkey also joined. Because of geography, Australia and New Zealand missed out on membership. In place of this, the ANZUS agreement was made by the United States with these nations.

4. The Truman Doctrine was an American foreign policy designed to contain communism by giving Greece and Turkey economic aid. Gaining the support of the Republicans who controlled Congress, President Harry S. Truman proclaimed the Doctrine on March 12, 1947. It stated that the United States would support Greece and Turkey with economic and military aid to prevent their falling into the Soviet sphere. The Doctrine shifted American foreign policy toward the Soviet Union from *Détente* to, as George F. Kennan phrased it, a policy of containment of Soviet expansion. Historians often use it to mark the starting date of the Cold War.

5. The Korean War, occurring between June 25, 1950, and a cease-fire on July 27, 1953, was a war fought in Korea that was divided by the post-World War II Soviet and American occupation zones, with large scale participation by other countries. The war began with the invasion of capitalist South Korea by forces in Communist North Korea in 1950 and ended as a stalemate between the sides in 1953.

The principal support on the side of the North was China, with limited assistance by Soviet combat advisors, military pilots, and weapons. South Korea was supported by UN forces, principally from the United States, although many other nations also contributed personnel. When the conflict began, North and South Korea existed as provisional governments competing for control over the Korean peninsula after the Division of Korea.

Thanks to a temporary Soviet absence from the Security Council—the Soviets were boycotting the Security Council to protest the exclusion of *People's Republic of China (PRC)* from the UN—there was no veto by Stalin and the (Nationalist controlled) Republic of China government held the Chinese seat. Without Soviet and Chinese vetoes, and with only Yugoslavia abstaining, the UN voted to aid South Korea on June 27. U.S. forces were joined by troops from 15 other UN members: Canada, Australia, New Zealand, Britain, France, South Africa, Turkey, Thailand, Greece, the Netherlands, Ethiopia, Colombia, the Philippines, Belgium, and Luxembourg.

The Soviet Union and its allies, however, challenged the resolution on grounds of illegality since a permanent member of the council (Soviet Union) was absent from the voting. The North Korean government also did not concur. In 1950, A Soviet resolution calling for an end of hostilities and withdrawal of foreign troops was rejected.

In South Korea, the war is often called 6.25, from the date of the start of the conflict or, more formally, Han-guk Jeonjaeng (literally "Korean War"). In North Korea, it is formally called the Fatherland Liberation War. In the United States, the conflict was officially termed a police action—the Korean Conflict—rather than a war, largely in order to avoid the necessity of a declaration of war by the U.S. Congress. The war is sometimes referred to outside Korea as "The Forgotten War" because it is a major conflict of the 20th century that garners far less attention than World War II, which preceded it, and the controversial Vietnam War, which succeeded it. In China, the conflict was known as the War to Resist America and Aid Korea, but is today commonly called the "Korean War."

6. The 1961 Bay of Pigs Invasion (also known in Cuba as the *Playa Girón* after the beach in the Bay of Pigs where the landing took place) was an unsuccessful U.S.-planned and funded attempted invasion by armed Cuban exiles in southwest Cuba. An attempt to overthrow the government of Fidel Castro, this action accelerated a rapid deterioration in Cuban–American relations, which was further worsened by the Cuban Missile Crisis the

following year. The name Bay of Pigs comes from Bahia de *Cochinos*, where in all probability *Cochino* refers to a species of Triggerfish (Balistes vetula), rather than pigs (Sus scrofa).

7. The Iran-Contra Affair was a political scandal in the United States during the 1980s. Large volumes of documents relating to the scandal were destroyed or withheld from investigators by Reagan administration officials. The affair is still shrouded with secrecy and it is very hard to discover the facts. It involved several members of the Reagan Administration, who in 1986 helped to illegally sell arms to Iran, an avowed enemy, and used the proceeds to fund, also illegally, the Contras, a right-wing guerrilla organization in Nicaragua.

   After the arms sales were revealed in November 1986, President Ronald Reagan appeared on national television and denied that they had occurred. However, a week later, on November 13, he returned to the airwaves to affirm that weapons were indeed transferred to Iran. He denied that they were part of an exchange for hostages.

8. The *Southeast Asia Treaty Organization (SEATO)*, created by the Southeast Asia Collective Defense Treaty or the Manila Pact, was an international organization for collective defense established on September 8, 1954. It was primarily created to block further communist gains in Southeast Asia. The organization's headquarters was located in Bangkok, Thailand. *SEATO* was dissolved on June 30, 1977.

   The *Central Treaty Organization* (also referred to as *CENTO*, original name was *Middle East Treaty Organization* or *METO*, also known as the Baghdad Pact) was adopted in 1955 by Iraq, Turkey, Pakistan, and Iran, as well as Turkey, Pakistan, and Iran, as well as the United Kingdom. Although American pressure, along with promises of military and economic largesse, were key in the negotiations leading to the agreement, the United States chose not to initially participate as to avoid alienating Arab states with which it was still attempting to cultivate friendly relations.

Some (particularly nationalist radicals) saw the Pact as an attempt by the British to retain influence in the Middle East as a substitute for the loss of their empire in India. In 1958 the United States joined the military committee of the alliance. It is generally viewed as one of the least successful of the Cold War alliances. Organizations headquarters were initially located in Baghdad (Iraq) 1955–1958 and Ankara (Turkey) 1958–1979.

Chapter 2

1. For a concise account of the efforts made by the nascent "India lobby" in the United States to persuade the organizers of the formative session of the United Nations Conference in San Francisco to replace the nominees to the conference provided by the British-dominated *Government of India (GOI)* with Vijayalakshmi Pandit of the Indian National Congress as the sole spokesperson for soon-to-be-independent India, see Chapter 10, pp. 379–386, "The India Lobby and the San Francisco Conference," in Harold A. Gould, *Sikhs, Swamis, Students and Spies: The Rise of the India Lobby in the United States, 1900 to 1946*, Sage India, 2006.

2. See Note 5, Chapter 1. The reason why the U.S. could be authorized by the UN to lead a "police action" against the North Korean invasion of the South was because the Soviet Union was boycotting the organization.

3. This was the book that profoundly influenced the evolution of postwar U.S. foreign policy toward the Middle East and South Asia. For background on Caroe's South Asia regional expertise and ideological predilections, see, Olaf Caroe, *The Pathans*. Karachi: Oxford University Press, 1958.

Chapter 3

1. There is veritable library of works on John Foster Dulles, which describe and analyse his political evolution as one of the principal architects of the Cold War. But for a single book which

traces the origins, character, and impact of John Foster Dulles and his two siblings, Allen and Eleanor Lansing Dulles, see: Mosley, *A Bibliography of Eleanor, Allen, and John Foster Dulles and Their Family Network*, (New York: The Dial Press, 1978).

2. The emergence and crystallization of Muslim political self-consciousness dates back to the turn of the century. It correlates with the rise of nationalism in India which itself was a byproduct of the pervasive institutional transformation taking place throughout the Subcontinent associated with the introduction of modernity. As modern organization gradually ramified throughout the Subcontinent, the British Raj found itself confronted with escalating demands for shared participation in the material benefits that modern technology was yielding. Because India is a highly pluralistic social world, political mobilization in pursuit of these demands were increasingly expressed in cultural-linguistic and ethno-religious terms. It is in this context that the Hindu–Muslim divide occurred which underlay the Partition of Bengal in 1905 and ultimately Partition in 1945 and the Kashmir dispute that quickly followed on its heels. There is a vast literature on this process of which the following citations are among the best:

Francis Robinson, *Separatism among Indian Muslims* (Cambridge: Cambridge University Press, 1974); Anil Seal, *The Emergence of Indian Nationalism: Competition Collaboration in the Later Nineteenth Century* (Cambridge: Cambridge University Press, 1968); John Gallagher, Gordon Johnson, and Anil Seal, *Locality, Province and Nation: Essays on Indian Politics, 1870–1940* (Cambridge: Cambridge University Press, 1973); Harold A. Gould, *Grass-Roots Politics in India: A Century of Political Evolution in Faizabad District* (New Delhi: Oxford & IBH, 1994).

3. This story has appeared in numerous sources. One of these is: Richard J. Barnet, *The Alliance: America, Europe, Japan, Makers of the Postwar World* (New York: Simon and Schuster, 1983), p. 34.

Chapter 4

1. Galbraith gives a good account of how the Chinese attack affect the U.S.–Indian relations.

Chapter 5

1. Harold Gould, LBJ Library, July, 1990.
2. Harold Gould, personal interview, 1987, Washington, DC, with source who wishes to remain anonymous.

Chapter 7

1. William Saxbe, personal interview, 1987.

Chapter 11

1. The *Comprehensive Test Ban Treaty (CTBT)*, which opened for signature in 1996, was intended to prohibit all nuclear test explosions. The *CTBT* has achieved near universal adherence; however, Article XIV of the Treaty requires ratification by 44 named states before the Treaty can enter into force.

   Of these 44 named states, three—India, Pakistan, North Korea—have not signed the Treaty. A further seven states—China, Columbia, Egypt, Indonesia, Iran, Israel, and the United States—have signed but not ratified the Treaty.

   Although the Bush administration is currently continuing with the 13 year-old nuclear test moratorium, it has made clear its opposition to the *CTBT*, and it is possible that the United States could resume nuclear explosions in the future.

References

Acheson Dean. 1950. *The Foreign Relations of the United States, 1947, Vol. 3.* Washington, DC: U.S. Government Printing Office.

———. 1969. *Present at the Creation: My Years in the State Department.* New York and London: W.W. Norton.

Barnet, Richard, J. 1983. *The Alliance: America, Europe, Japan, Makers of the Postwar World.* NewYork: Simon and Schuster.

Bjorkmanm, James Warner. 1980. "Public Law 480 and the Policies of Self-Help and Short-Tether: Indo-American Relations, 1965–69," in Lloyd and Susanne Rudolph, *The Regional Imperative.* Atlantic Highlands, New Jersey: The Humanities Press.

Bowles, Chester. 1951. *Ambassador's Report.* London: Victor Gollancz.

Burki, Shahid, Javed. 1980. *Bhutto, 1971–1977.* London: Macmillan.

Caroe, Olaf. 1958. *The Pathans.* Karachi: Oxford University Press.

Cohen, Stephen Philip. 1992. "The Reagan Administration and India," in Harold A. Gould and Sumit Ganguly (eds), *The Hope and the Reality: U.S.–Indian Relations from Roosevelt to Reagan,* pp. 139–154. Boulder, CO: Westview Press.

Galbraith, John K. 1969. *Ambassador's Journal: A Personal Account of the Kennedy Years.* New York: Houghton Mifflin.

Gallagher, John, Gordon Johnson, and Anil Seal. 1973. *Locality, Province and Nation: Essays on Indian Politics, 1870–1940.* Cambridge: Cambridge University Press.

Ganguly, Sumit. 1992. "US–Indian Relations during the Lyndon Johnson Era," in Harold. A. Gould and Sumit Ganguly (eds), *The Hope and the Reality: US–Indian Relations from Roosevelt to Reagan,* pp. 81–90. Boulder, CO: Westview Press.

Goheen, F. Robert. 1992. "U.S. Policy During the Carter Admin-istration," in Harold A. Gould and Sumit Ganguly (eds), *The Hope and the Reality: U.S.–Indian Relations from Roosevelt to Reagan*, pp. 121–138. Boulder, CO: Westview Press.

Goodwin, Doris Kearns. 1976/1991. "The Vice Presidency," in *Lyndon Johnson and the American Dream*, pp. 160–169. New York: St. Martin's Griffin.

Gould, Harold A. 1990. Private research in LBJ Library, Austin, Texas.

———. 1994. *Grass-Roots Politics in India: A Century of Political Evolution in Faizabad District*. New Delhi: Oxford & IBH.

———. 2001. "The Reasons Why: The U.S. Failure to Control the Nuclear Agenda in South Asia," in A. Kapur, Y.K. Malik, H.A. Gould, and A.G. Rubinoff (eds), *India and the United States in a Changing World*, pp. 144–215. New Delhi: Sage Publications.

———. 2006. "The India Lobby and the San Francisco Conference," in *Sikhs, Swamis, Students and Spies: The Rise of the India Lobby in the United States, 1900 to 1946*, pp. 379–386. New Delhi: Sage Publications.

Haqqani, Husain. 2005. *Pakistan: Between Mosque and Military*. Washington, DC: Carnegie Endowment for International Peace.

———. 2006. "Pakistan's Perennial Political Crisis," *The State of Pakistan*," The publication of papers presented on April 2, 2006, at a colloquium organized by the South Asia Program of the Paul H. Nitze School of Advanced International Studies, John Hopkins University, Washington, DC, pp. 3–17.

Hardgraves, Robert. 1993. "Alliance Politics and Minority Govern-ment: India at the Polls, 1989 and 1991," in Harold A. Gould and Sumit Ganguly (eds), *India Votes: Alliance Politics in the Ninth and Tenth General Elections*, pp. 291–293. Boulder, CO: Westview Press.

Hitchens, Christopher. 2001. *The Trial of Henry Kissinger*. New York: Verso.

Kennedy, John F. 1956. *Profiles in Courage*. New York: Harper & Brothers.

Kissinger, Henry. 1979. *The White House Years*. Boston: Little, Brown.

Kux, Dennis. 1993. *India and the United States: Estranged Democracies*. Washington, DC: National Defense University.

———. 2001. *The United States and Pakistan: 1947–2000*. Washington, DC: The Woodrow Wilson Center.

McMahon, Robert J. 1994. *The Cold War on the Periphery: The United States, India and Pakistan*. New York: Columbia University Press.

Mosley, Leonard. 1978. *Dulles: A Bibliography of Eleanor, Allen and John Foster Dulles and Their Family Network*. New York: The Dial Press.

Robinson, Francis. 1974. *Separatism among Indian Muslims*. Cambridge: Cambridge University Press.

Rubinoff, G. Arthur. 2001. "Legislative Perceptions of Indo-American Relations", in A. Kapur, Y.K. Malik, H.A. Gould, and A.G. Rubinoff (eds), *India and the United States in a Changing World*, pp. 199–200. New Delhi: Sage Publications.

Rudolph, Llyod. 1993. "Why Rajiv Gandhi's Death Saved the Congress: How an Event Affected the Outcome of the 1991 Election in India," in Harold A. Gould and Sumit Ganguly (eds), *India Votes: Alliance Politics in the Ninth and Tenth General Elections*, pp. 436–453. Boulder, CO: Westview Press.

Seal, Anil. 1968. *The Emergence of Indian Nationalism: Competition Collaboration in the Later Nineteenth Century*. Cambridge: Cambridge University Press.

Schlesinger, Arthur M. Jr. 1967. *A Thousand Days: John F. Kennedy in the White House*. New York: Mayflower-Dell Paperback.

Schaffer, Howard. 1993. *Chester Bowles, New Dealer in the Cold War*. Cambridge, MA: Harvard University Press.

Tahir-Kehli, Shirin. 1997. *India, Pakistan and the United States: Breaking with the Past.* New York: Council on Foreign Relations.

Talbott, Strobe. 2004. *Engaging India: Diplomacy, Democracy, and the Bomb.* Washington, DC: Brookings Institution Press.

Thornton, Thomas. 1992. "U.S.–Indian Relations in the Nixon and Ford Years," in Harold A. Gould and Sumit Ganguly (eds), *The Hope and the Reality: U.S.–Indian Relations from Roosevelt to Reagan.* Boulder, CO: Westview Press.

Index

About the Author

Harold A. Gould is a Visiting Professor in the Center for South Asian Studies at the University of Virginia. Previous to that he was Professor of Anthropology and Director of the Center for Asian Studies at the University of Illinois in Champaign-Urbana. He received his Ph.D. in Anthropology at Washington University of St. Louis in 1959. Since going to India on a Fulbright Scholarship in 1954–1955, Dr Gould has made numerous research trips to India (with grants from the National Science Foundation, the National Institute of Mental Health, the American Institute of Indian Studies, and the University of Illinois Research Board); he spent more than a total of ten years in the country spread over more than fifty years. His research and scholarly publications encompass every facet of Indian society and civilization that is relevant for a social scientist/social historian, including rural society, social stratification, local-level politics, electoral processes, and national and international politics.